COUPLES THERAPY WORKBOOK:

Essential Skills For Communication, Rebuilding Trust, Emotional and Physical Connection and Much More A Relationship Workbook for Couples

TABLE OF CONTENTS

INTRODUCTION

Marriage is a sacred union between two individuals who have chosen to commit to each other emotionally, physically, and spiritually. It is a social, religious, and cultural institution that has existed in various forms across different cultures and societies throughout human history.

Many believe marriage is a unique and special commitment because it involves a deep emotional, physical, and spiritual intimacy between two people. It can create a sense of security and stability to help couples navigate life's challenges together.

In a world filled with problems, distractions, and stressors, it's inevitable to experience different kinds of relationship problems, either financial, mental, or physical. Unfortunately, in many cases, partners would give up on their relationship and end it when things get difficult, putting them and their significant other in more pain than expected. Some of the common challenges that arise in a marriage include:

Communication Issues: Communication is an essential part of any relationship, and when it breaks down, it can lead to misunderstandings, conflict, and resentment.

Financial Issues: Money matters can be a significant source of conflict in a marriage, such as disagreements over spending habits, debt, or financial goals.

Infidelity: When one partner engages in an extramarital affair, it can be a devastating blow to the trust and intimacy of the relationship.

Parenting Conflicts: Raising children can be a rewarding experience, but it can also bring up disagreements over parenting styles, discipline, and other aspects of child-rearing.

Differences in Values or Interests: When partners have significant differences in their beliefs, values, or interests, it can create tension and conflict in the relationship.

Intimacy Issues: A lack of physical or emotional intimacy can be a source of frustration and dissatisfaction in a marriage.

Power Struggles: When partners have different levels of control or decision-making power in the relationship, it can lead to power issues and resentment.

Stress and Life Changes: Life changes, such as job loss, illness, or relocation, can put a strain on a marriage, leading to discontentment and stress.

One of the most recommended ways to work through these issues is couples therapy, a specialized form designed to help couples resolve conflicts, improve communication, and strengthen their relationship. It's useful for couples experiencing difficulties in their relationship, such as communication issues, infidelity, intimacy problems, etc.

The counseling aims to help couples gain insight into their relationship and develop the skills and strategies they need to overcome their challenges. A qualified marriage counselor or therapist can help couples identify the underlying issues causing problems in their relationship and work with them to develop effective solutions.

It involves a series of structured sessions conducted by a trained professional. During these sessions, the counselor or therapist will work with the couple to identify the issues causing problems in their relationship, explore different perspectives, and develop strategies for improving and strengthening their bond.

One of the most recommended therapies is the Gottman method which is built on the notion that every couple has a "Sound Relationship House" built on trust, dedication, and mutual goals.

WEEK 1: OVERVIEW OF THE GOTTMAN METHOD

Developed by Doctors John and Julie Gottman, this comprehensive and empirical therapy has been helping couples for over four decades. This approach aims to help couples improve their problem-solving skills and emotional intelligence, which are vital to promoting communication and understanding in a relationship.

The Gottmans' decades of research showed that communication and behavioral patterns determine relational success. To ensure relationship success, the Gottman method aims to build trust, emotional intimacy, commitment, and goal-setting by understanding the root causes of a problem and building comprehensive solutions to solve them while providing the couple with the skills to build their relationship.

The Gottmans proposed seven principles to help couples achieve a sound and stable relationship:

Enhancing Love Maps

When you decide to spend your life with someone, it would be like giving someone a map of your inner world; this includes your likes, dislikes, goals, and perspectives – everything your partner needs to know about you. The goal of enhancing your love maps is to keep building up and nourishing your relationship. When roots and boundaries are set and established, they will guide you and your significant other into a secure and strong partnership. With a love map, couples can easily solve problems and surpass difficulties without the risk of falling out.

Promoting Admiration

Admiration is not just about someone's fondness and love but also mutual respect between partners. One of the reasons many relationships fail is one's inability to fully accept their partner, leading them to change how their partner thinks and acts because they do not fit the criteria. Chances are, the partner would feel chained in the relationship because of all the restrictions, leading them to feel less confident. Through promoting admiration, one can understand what their mate stands for regarding their dreams, families, and career without imposing and turning them into someone they don't like.

Turning toward each other

In any relationship, disagreements are inevitable, so it is important to always turn toward each other rather than away. One of the common mistakes couples make is that they start to see each other as the enemy when they should be looking at the main problem as the enemy. By changing their mindset, they will be able to solve the problem as a team, thinking of each other's best interests.

Having a positive perspective

This principle is about keeping a balanced and positive outlook on the relationship. It involves focusing on the good in the relationship and recognizing that all relationships have ups and downs. By keeping a positive perspective, couples can maintain a sense of hope and optimism, even during difficult times.

Managing conflicts

Many couples shy away from speaking out about something that bothers them in the relationship, fearing it may cause conflict. Little do they know that keeping your problems to yourself leads to pent-up emotions and fallout. The Gottman method encourages couples to open up about their grievances in a relationship, even if it causes conflict. The main goal is to fix the disagreement through a healthy conversation to create the necessary steps to manage the problem.

Helping each other achieve goals

Each partner has individual goals, even if they are in a partnership. Even if one doesn't completely understand the reason for the other's aspirations, the goal is to support and uplift your partner, even if it's difficult. An example of that scenario would be someone who wants to join the army, their partner would definitely be anxious about this goal, yet it's still important to help and support them through their journey.

Creating Shared Meaning

The final principle of the Gottman Method is about creating shared meaning in the relationship, which means finding common values, beliefs, and goals the couple can share and work towards together. This way, couples can develop a deeper sense of connection and purpose, helping them build a sound relationship house.

Phases of Gottman Therapy Method:

Gottman Method is a systematic and research-based approach to couples therapy in three phases: Assessment, Intervention, and Follow-Up.

Assessment Phase

The Gottman Method's first step is gathering information about the couple using a series of questionnaires and interview questions to understand their relationship history, current relationship issues, and goals for therapy. The therapist may also facilitate activities to observe how they think and behave. This information is used to develop a personalized treatment plan to solve the problems and determine the necessary skills to make these solutions sustainable.

Intervention Phase

This next phase involves the couple trying the therapist's strategies to determine how they could be incorporated into the relationship. The intervention phase is not straightforward; it entails a trial and error of methods that could help the relationship work. After every session, the therapist will assign the couple some activities they need to apply in a week, and they need to share how it worked during their next meeting. Whichever strategies work best should be applied by the couple even after therapy.

Follow-up Phase

The last phase entails scheduling follow-up meetings after the main therapy to determine how sustainable the solutions are and if they could find better ways to improve the relationship. By scheduling follow-up meetings, the therapist can help the couple through any difficulty adjusting to the new process, plus it helps them mitigate issues even before they arise.

Overall, the Gottman Method is a comprehensive and evidence-based approach to couples therapy that helps couples create a sound relationship house. And as you can observe, the Gottman method's efficacy boils down to an important element – communication. Sadly, many people often disregard this concept, and its importance is undermined. Little do they know there is more to communication than just speaking and listening. By learning how to communicate properly, people have a greater chance at success in every aspect of life, including relationships. In this next chapter, let's discuss communication and how to build the skill to improve it.

Communication

Communication entails exchanging information, ideas, and thoughts between two or more individuals, allowing us to express ourselves, understand others, and build connections. In a relationship, communication enables you to express your goals, needs, wants, and feelings and strengthens the bond between you and your partner.

However, communication is not merely stating words; a good partnership requires effective communication, a combination of strategies crucial to prevent misunderstandings, disagreements, and conflict. Given that all relationships have ups and downs, a good communication style can help you deal with disagreements and forge a stronger, healthier relationship.

Benefits of Effective Communication in Relationships

To better understand how essential effective communication is, here are seven important benefits of effective communication:

1. It promotes mutual respect

Effective communication between partners enables both parties to grow to respect one another. No matter how different their perspectives can be, the understanding and empathy they show one another matter. Whenever disagreements arise, having mutual respect allows partners to listen and communicate with an open heart and mind, to avoid offending or blatantly hurting the other.

Mutual respect will help build your relationship by going through conflicts because your partner might have insights you weren't anticipating. But more than that, it shows that you value them highly enough to consider how something can affect them and that you are sincere enough to be upfront.

2. It Eliminates Uncertainty

According to Mark Twain, "If you tell the truth, you don't have to recall anything,"

One of the main issues in relationships is withholding information because of the fear that the other might get hurt or mad. By telling white lies and eliminating details, people stress over recalling their reasons for doing this, which could lead to more lies until it eventually unfolds, hurting one's partner deeply.

Gaining better communication skills will allow you to open your mind without the fear of being rejected and the fear of hurting your partner. Effective communication lets you know how to reveal your thoughts straightforwardly and respectfully in a way your partner would appreciate.

3. It Assists in Preventing Misunderstandings

No matter how close people get in a romantic relationship, they must realize that they're still different individuals with different personalities and perspectives hence, the occasional miscommunications. Other times, we fail to communicate crucial information, which causes the complex gears of our connection to jam.

Simply put, communicating helps to avoid misunderstandings. Fewer things remain unsaid when we express ourselves freely to those we love. This way, we grow accustomed to communicating concepts and ideas in an understandable manner to others.

Overall, the people we care about start to count on us to tell them the truth. When you aren't concerned about saying the wrong thing, the pressure is off, and the relationship is much healthier.

4. It Promotes Trust

Building trust takes time. It is a long-term process that entails open and honest communication with your partner. If one doesn't know how to communicate effectively, it's difficult to trust them because you never know whether they're speaking the truth or saying what they truly mean. This doubt is why couples need to learn effective communication. Hence, they know how to communicate their thoughts and feelings clearly.

5. It Allows Partners to Support One Another

Issues arise when people don't share their struggles and grievances with their significant other. It is important to remain open when facing personal difficulties so your partner can support you, even if you think they can't help. They can lend you a shoulder, which is wonderful, but they'll also gain the satisfaction of knowing they contributed to your progress.

Remember that nothing will improve if your partner is unaware of the problem. Instead, you'll each be the support the other needs if you can strengthen your two-way communication.

6. It Fosters Love Between Couples

This euphemism will sound cliché, but love is like a flower; it must be watered regularly. So likewise, our love may get malnourished if we allow our communication to stagnate.

If we cease talking with someone, we can't expect to continue to gain their love. Regrettably, sometimes, when a relationship's love simply dwindles, you cannot bring it back.

But in most cases, what's lacking is open communication, the kind that initially made you fall in love. You must be able to remind one another of the reasons you fell in love because this allows you to always look for the positive things in your relationship when things don't go well.

7. It Improves Your Mood

Sharing your preferences and goals with someone is one of the most precious gifts in any relationship. Genuine happiness can act as an echo chamber when a person has a partner with whom they communicate well.

We communicate our emotions effortlessly when our partner is open and genuine. And when we do that, both sides benefit from the joy.

Openly expressing your happiness to another person creates a happy atmosphere that encourages the spread of more of the same. This concept is a built-in relationship enhancer and a more wholesome method of handling our feelings.

Barriers to Communication:

People say that building skills for effective communication is easy. Little do they know that it is filled with challenges called communication barriers. The most common forms of barriers include language, noise, semantics, psychological, and personal barriers.

Language barriers arise when two people speak different languages, making it difficult to understand one another. Noise barriers, on the other hand, occur when two people cannot hear each other well due to loud and disturbing noises in their surroundings.

Semantic barriers, however, arise when a person uses the wrong jargon, faulty analogies, translations, body language, and gestures in communicating. An example would be using the OK sign with your thumb up; while in many countries, such as the United States, this gesture means okay, some countries find it offensive. And for that reason, it's important to research the culture of the person you are talking to.

Next, psychological barriers include when a person has mental health issues, learning difficulties, and mental delays. When communicating with people with these disabilities, it is important to show them patience because of the barrier they cannot escape.

Lastly, personal barriers, they are the worst type, leading to distressing conflicts and misunderstandings. Most of the time, they lead to fallout in relationships because of the impact of one's personal thoughts, attitudes, behaviors and feelings. People who have personal barriers would show the following bad habits in a relationship:

1. The Silent Treatment

The silent treatment is a technique people use to control a situation, and it may even be a manipulation strategy. This pattern occurs when someone refuses to talk to the person completely, not even recognizing their presence. It creates a strong barrier that could lead to pent-up emotions, separation anxiety, and other emotional problems.

2. Insulting remarks and hurtful language

People use verbal statements to harm their partners and defend their feelings when they are hurt during an argument.

Some degrading sentiments that are commonly used in relationships include:

- You are useless.
- You are nothing.
- You will never achieve your dreams.
- That's why no one likes you.
- You are weak.

Some people would brush this off like it's normal in a relationship, but it is considered a form of verbal abuse.

3. Screaming and Yelling

When couples communicate by yelling and raising their voices, the message gets lost in the noise, and new problems arise that cause the pair to lose focus on the initial argument or issue. What matters is the tone you use, not what you say.

4. Not communicating what you need

Assuming your partner is aware of and comprehends your thoughts without sharing them will only lead to unfulfilled needs, hurt feelings, and a total lack of understanding. No one is fed if their mouth is shut. The person with unmet requirements must effectively communicate those wants to improve the likelihood that their partner will recognize and fulfill those needs.

5. Half-listening

It is never a good idea to hear only a portion of the message; focusing on your partner's words is extremely important, especially during arguments. By half-listening, it will be difficult for couples to figure out a solution to their problem, or worse, it could aggravate the situation.

6. Wrong timing

There will always be a time and place for communicating sensitive things to your spouse. One of the most common issues people can observe is couples fighting in public. This situation could involve exchanging painful remarks and criticisms which is humiliating to both parties. Even if your partner does something wrong, it is important to take them somewhere private where both of you can discuss the problem without any audience; this would save your partner from further embarrassment.

7. Assumptions and Criticisms

One needs to understand that there are always two sides to every story. Both sides must be heard before someone reacts and assumes the worst. This dilemma usually happens in a community where rumors spread easily. Gossipmongers could tell stories and lies about partners, often leading to misunderstandings. If a couple is a victim of false accusations, working through it as a team without jumping to conclusions is super important. It is important to validate the information one is receiving before making any judgment.

8. Gaslighting

Gaslighting occurs when someone tries to manipulate a victim's perception of reality. This happens when a person hurts the other and denies that it happened to say that the victim is lying and imagining the whole thing. Another scenario of gaslighting is when you hurt your partner, then keep saying that it's their fault they are feeling hurt because they are sensitive. If one is a constant victim of gaslighting, they start questioning their sanity, stripping them of their confidence, and leaving them feeling worthless.

Effects of Poor Communication

Depression

Depression is not just sadness; it is a number of symptoms, such as irritation, exhaustion, trouble focusing, changes in eating or sleep habits, feelings of helplessness or unworthiness, a decrease in enjoyment of routine tasks, and occasionally suicidal thoughts are present.

It's possible to develop clinical depression, usually referred to as serious depression, if you suffer five or more symptoms for at least two weeks. For the sake of both your relationship and your own health, you should seek emergency medical or mental-health evaluation for this serious situation.

Some of the signs of depression in relationships include reduced sex drive. According to psychologists, your libido typically declines along with your mood when it does. Since sex is often the glue that holds relationships together, if your partner doesn't understand why you haven't been intimate recently, they might assume you have lost interest in them or no longer care.

You fight more when you are depressed because you are not only in a constant cycle of sadness but also feel irritable, angry, and cynical, which causes conflicts. Chances are, you would want to isolate yourself from the world. You no longer want to leave the house or meet your friends and family, plus you slowly lose interest in the things you used to love. People might think that you are giving up control when in reality, nothing makes sense to you anymore, so you lose all motivation and inspiration to keep moving forward. In this case, it is important to see an expert before any of the symptoms escalate.

Anxiety

Anxiety in relationships is the constant feeling of concern, insecurity, and uncertainty, possibly because of ineffective and hurtful communication. Because of the emotional trauma that hurtful words cause, one might feel doubtful that their partner still loves them. It also leads people to think about whether they still matter, or are still loved, if their partner wants to be in a long-term relationship or break up.

Without treatment, a person with anxiety could develop negative behaviors such as ignoring their partner's bad behaviors because they become afraid of starting a conflict when they call them out. In addition, anxious people opt to miss out on new activities and opportunities because they fear any hurtful things their partner might say to them. In consequence, they end up slowly sabotaging themselves.

Antagonism

Another effect of poor communication is tormenting one another. Instead of having a peaceful relationship, a partner could end up being their worst enemy. This pattern entails daily insults, criticisms, and blame.

Disconnection

If these signs of poor communication persist, over time, there will be a disconnect between partners, leading to a fallout. They would soon realize that their relationship is irreparable, and they would opt to move on rather than continue destroying themselves in the relationship.

Toxic Relationship

Where there is poor communication, expect a high chance that a relationship could turn toxic. Over time, the couple might resort to various forms of manipulation to get what they want from their partners instead of communicating with them properly. These strategies include blackmail, humiliation, gaslighting, abuse, etc. It could even lead to sabotage, which could be very dangerous among couples and those around them.

Poor communication in relationships leads to stress, so it's important to learn how to communicate properly and respectfully with your partner. Not only will this help you bond and get to know one another, but it also allows you to build mutual trust and respect, which are important pillars in having a sound relationship house.

Communication Styles

Now that we have discussed the importance of effective communication, it is time to understand how you can improve your communication skills. But before that, what do you think is your communication style? By understanding this, you will have a clearer understanding of what to improve.

Here are the four communication styles:

Passive

People who communicate in a passive manner tend to behave carelessly and submit to anyone, even without reason. They typically don't express their demands or sentiments, allowing others to decide and talk for them. You can also observe a lack of external communication, frequently resulting in misunderstanding or resentment.

Some signs indicating passive communication include eye contact avoidance, bad posture, and people-pleasing. Passive people are also inclined to convey that "people never consider my sentiments."

Examples of passive phrases:

"It isn't that important."

"I only want to maintain peace."

"It doesn't matter."

"Just leave it alone."

Aggressive

When someone communicates aggressively, it is frequently clear. You'll notice this method through signs, such as speaking with a loud and demanding voice, maintaining close eye contact, and dominating or controlling others by accusing, frightening, criticizing, threatening, or attacking them.

The following are some examples of phrases that an aggressive communicator might use:

"You're wrong, and I'm right."

"No matter what, I'll get my way."

"It is entirely your fault."

Passive-Aggressive

Users of the passive-aggressive communication style may appear passive on the outside. Still, they may feel helpless or trapped, developing animosity that causes them to seethe or act subtly, covertly, or vaguely.

Most people who communicate passive-aggressively would grumble to themselves rather than confront someone. They struggle to convey their emotions, exhibit non-congruent facial expressions, and occasionally even downplay the severity of the situation.

The most common ways that passive-aggressive communicators express themselves to others are through body language or a lack of open communication, such as giving someone the silent treatment, spreading rumors behind others' backs, or undermining other people's efforts. Despite appearing cooperative, passive-aggressive communicators may secretly act oppositely.

In the end, passive-aggressive communicators are conscious of their wants but occasionally find it difficult to express them.

A passive-aggressive communicator might employ the following phrases:

"I don't mind, but don't be shocked if someone else becomes upset."

"Sure, we can do things your way, but let's be honest—that's a dumb idea."

Assertive

The assertive communication style, considered the most effective, promotes an open line of communication while remaining nonobtrusive. When expressing their needs, wants, opinions, and feelings, assertive communicators consider the feelings of others. When communicating assertively, one balances their rights with the rights of others such that both parties benefit from the conversation.

An assertive communicator might use the following statements:

"We all have the right to express ourselves to one another appropriately ."

"I am aware that I have options in life, and I weigh them."

"I respect other people's rights,"

Have you determined your communication style so far? Whatever the case is, there will always be room for improvement. Here are some effective ways to do so:

Improve Your Communication Skills

1. Use active listening techniques

When it's time to listen to your partner, be present, attentive, and concentrated. One way to show your partner you are listening is through active listening.

To effectively communicate, one must listen to another person's words while attempting to understand their meaning and intent.

To actively listen to someone means participating actively in the conversation, demonstrating attention by maintaining eye contact, observing (and making use of) nonverbal cues, posing open-ended inquiries to elicit additional responses, reiterating what has been said and paraphrasing it, listening to understand rather than to answer, and withholding opinions and guidance.

Seven Active Listening Strategies

The word "active" suggests that as you listen to people, you act in a way that makes them feel heard and understood. Reaching this state calls for seven tactics that can help you promote active listening in relationships.

1. Be Fully Present

Being fully present during a conversation is necessary for active listening because it allows you to pay close attention to what is being said using all of your senses, including sight and sound.

Put your phone aside, eliminate distractions, stop daydreaming, and silence your inner voice to maximize this active listening approach's merits. Instead, keep your attention on your conversation partner and let the rest of the world fade away.

2. Take Note of Nonverbal Cues

65% of communication between people is nonverbal, which includes gestures, eye contact, and body language. Observing these nonverbal clues can reveal much about a person and what they are attempting to communicate. For instance, if they speak quickly, this can indicate that they are agitated or frightened. They can be drowsy or try to select their words if they speak slowly and carefully. If they say they are okay, but you can observe tension in their body, it could mean they are lying about being okay.

Your nonverbal cues during active listening are just as crucial. Use open, non-threatening body language to convey to the other person that you are attentive. This entails keeping your arms open, leaning in, and nodding at significant moments. You must also consider your facial expressions to avoid sending the wrong message.

3. Maintain Eye Contact

Making eye contact is especially crucial when actively listening; it lets the other person know you are paying attention to and present during their speech. Additionally, it demonstrates that you are not being sidetracked by anything nearby.

However, you want to avoid making so much eye contact, which could turn the conversation awkward. Follow the 50/70 rule to avoid this situation, making eye contact for 50% to 70% of the listening time, sustaining the gaze for four to five seconds, and then glancing away momentarily.

4. Pose open-ended inquiries

Dead-end replies are frequently obtained from "yes or no" queries. This pattern prevents the conversation from moving along while actively listening, which is not what we want here. It also makes paying attention to what the other person is saying challenging because a succinct, non-descriptive response only offers a little insight.

Ask open-ended queries as an alternative to demonstrate your interest in the topic and the other person. You can use open-ended questions like these while actively listening:

- Please, explain that to me.
- What do you think about that?
- What do you consider to be the best going forward?
- What other ways do you think you could have reacted?

Open-ended inquiries promote thorough, in-depth responses, which is why mental health therapists frequently utilize them.

5. Reflect What You Hear

This technique entails paraphrasing what your partner said to ensure that you understand them correctly, plus it also makes them feel valued and heard.

Say something like, "In other words, what you are saying is that you are frustrated," or "I'm hearing that you are frustrated about this scenario," as an example. Then, give the person a chance to comment on how you paraphrased their statements, and let them continue.

Ask for clarification if necessary to better grasp something the other person has said; however, avoid getting caught up in the little print to the point where you overlook the bigger picture.

6. Have patience

Having patience allows your partner to speak uninterrupted. It entails refraining from filling pauses with your own ideas or stories. It also involves listening intently to comprehend rather than to speak. Avoid composing your response while the other person is still speaking. Additionally, don't change the subject suddenly because this suggests impatience and boredom.

Instead of interjecting your thoughts and opinions on what is being stated during active listening, you are there to serve as a sounding board.

7. Delay Judgment

The ability for the other person to feel comfortable sharing their thoughts depends on your ability to remain impartial and nonjudgmental in your comments. It creates a safe environment where partners know they won't be shamed, ridiculed, held accountable, or treated poorly.

Being less critical when listening involves demonstrating sympathy for the individual or their situation, gaining knowledge of various cultures and people, learning to accept others, realizing when you might be condemning someone else, and finally stopping those thoughts.

What does active listening look like? Here is an illustration of a conversation when multiple active listening strategies are employed.

Lisa: Hey, I just wanted to open up about something that's been bothering me for a while now.

Ralph: Sure, honey. Tell me, what's going on?

Lisa: This started when we were deciding on what to do for our anniversary dinner. I didn't feel like I was being heard. You kept mumbling about what you wanted to do as if you didn't want to consider some of my suggestions.

Ralph: Sorry I made you feel that way. It must be crushing to feel that you aren't heard about our anniversary preparations.

Lisa: It's just that I've put in so much effort in buying everything we need for the celebration I wanted, and I thought we could use some of them.

Ralph: I feel that it's not too late to use the things you bought to design our house. Do you already have a plan for getting started on the party?

Lisa: I do, yes. Do you have any other ideas we can add to the plan?

Ralph: Let's take some time to think together; I'm sure you and I can work things out. And I'm sorry for making you feel unheard. It was not my intention as I have been very excited. I didn't notice I was rambling.

Lisa: Thank you for seeing where I'm coming from. It made me feel better.

2. Speak Concisely

Aside from active listening, you must practice speaking clearly to communicate effectively. As much as possible, avoid using vague words to describe what you're feeling; otherwise, you will not get the desired results. For example, instead of saying, "I'm upset that you didn't do what I asked yesterday," you can say,

"I'm upset that you did not buy me flowers." By giving your partner specific reasons for your displeasure, they can better understand what you need and do it in the future.

3. Use "I" Statements

In therapy, mental health professionals frequently advise clients to communicate with others using "I" statements. This method is particularly popular in marriage counseling since it can be easy for couples to go into a never-ending cycle of blaming without ever addressing the underlying emotions or attachment problems that may be the root of their problems. By using "I" statements, couples may be able to communicate their ideas and feelings to one another without blaming the other or adding to the tension in their relationship.

Early in marital counseling, some couples could misuse "I" expressions. Someone could say to their partner, "I hate it when you don't listen to me," as an example. This sentence begins with "I"; however, it could be considered accusatory and may not be the best method to communicate one's feelings. A better way to express this would be, "I feel ignored and hated when you do not listen to what I am saying." Therefore, therapists frequently work with the patients they are caring for to practice proper "I" statements and investigate responses to the emotions that these statements convey.

How to Use "I" Messages?

Using "I" statements is not always common, and it frequently takes considerable effort to do so successfully. Nevertheless, here are some examples of conversations one can use the "I" statements correctly:

Scenario 1:

Common response: You constantly undermine what I say.

"I" Statement: I feel frustrated when you do not listen to what I say.

Scenario 2:

Common response: I hate it when you don't do what I say.

"I" Statement: I feel ignored when you don't do the simple things I request.

As you can observe, it allows people to express their thoughts and emotions respectfully, reducing the tendency of miscommunication and escalation of conflict.

4. Use Constructive Response

Active constructive response, also known as (ACR), involves providing a good response to positive news. According to one research, there are four approaches that people use to respond to good news:

1. Total disinterest – this includes paying little attention and changing the subject of discussion are examples of passive destructive behaviors. The common behaviors include turning back or sighing.

2. The ability to be constructively involved without any feeling of enthusiasm or happiness.

You may observe the person using a head nod and a soft grin as body language, for instance, "That's nice, baby."

3. Actively undermining the "positive" news by pointing out its flaws, casting doubt on the situation, and ending any sense of anticipation.

They may come off as reactive or combative with authoritarian body language.

You may hear, "Wow, are you sure you want to go there? It's so dangerous—have you considered the risks?" as an example.

4. Active, constructive traits. This approach involves actively reacting to the good news with interest and zeal, asking questions that assist in almost reliving the event, and the conversation is pleasant for both parties. This is how one should react to good news in a relationship.

The body language you should employ includes: leaning into the conversation, increased movement and hand gestures, and possibly showing something on the phone to express an emotion.

For example, you could say, "That's great. I'm very happy for you. What will happen next?"

By using ACR in responding to positive news, psychologists report increased self-confidence, intimacy, dedication, and relationship stability.

In conclusion, the Gottman method is based on understanding the main roots of a problem and determining the necessary skills and strategies to fix them. One of the most important skills to help couples achieve a sound relationship house is effective communication. By practicing this skill, people can gear their relationship to withstand the most difficult problems without instilling doubt, fear, and sadness in the relationship. By employing effective communication, partners work as a team in problem-solving to achieve their shared goals and maintain a stable and happy relationship.

Homework:

In this week's exercises, you will begin to explore the different types of communication and how they can affect your relationship. You will also learn about common communication barriers and how to overcome them.

Take the time to reflect on your communication style. How do you typically express yourself? Are there any barriers to communication that you have experienced in your relationship?

Practice active listening with your partner. Take turns sharing your thoughts, feelings, and experiences every day, and make sure to give your full attention to the other person when they are speaking.

Try using reflective listening when your partner is speaking. Repeat to them what they have said, in your own words, to ensure that you have understood their message correctly.

Show empathy towards your partner. Try to understand and share their feelings and respond in a way that supports and validates their needs and feelings.

Practice self-awareness by taking the time to understand your thoughts, feelings, and behaviors and how they may impact your communication with your partner.

WEEK 2: UNDERSTANDING EMOTIONS

Emotions give meaning to events; that is why people remember when a child is born, when someone dies, and when someone gets married – all of these events entail a specific emotion that will linger for life. Whether the emotion is positive or negative, it gives life purpose and makes it more colorful.

An emotional reaction is a response that people experience toward a certain situation or event. It stems from a person's emotions, which can be categorized into primary and secondary emotions. Primary or basic emotions include general feelings, such as happiness, sadness, anger, fear, surprise, and disgust. Secondary emotions are more complex because they are more specific than basic emotions. For example, under happiness, a person could feel excitement or love, and under anger, a person could feel jealousy or contempt.

It's also important to note that emotions are complex and can often overlap or interact with each other in subtle and nuanced ways. For example, a person may simultaneously feel happiness and sadness or anger and fear in response to a particular situation. An example of that predicament would be resigning from a toxic job; a person would be happy to be out of the company while still feeling sad because they will be leaving their coworkers behind.

In summary, life cannot exist without emotion. Whether it is happiness, anger, sadness, disgust, or fear, all these emotions have a purpose. One of the common mistakes that people make is undermining the effects of their emotions, which could lead to chaos and disaster. By understanding what emotions are, people can determine what affects them, why they are important, and what their role in our lives is. These concepts are what we are going to tackle in this chapter.

Emotions, Feelings, and Mood

Emotions, feelings, and moods are often interchanged because people think they're the same, but they are actually distinct concepts.

Emotions are brief, intense, and specific physiological and psychological responses to a particular event or stimulus, like, feeling anxious before a public speaking engagement or feeling happy when seeing a loved one. Emotions are often associated with physical sensations, such as heart rate or breathing changes, and can be expressed through behaviors such as facial expressions or body language.

On the other hand, feelings are subjective and often less intense experiences that are more long-lasting than emotions. Feelings are the interpretations of emotions; shaped by our beliefs, values, and past experiences. For example, feeling sad after the death of a loved one or feeling proud of a personal accomplishment because people are shaped to feel this way during such an event.

Lastly, the mood is a more general and long-lasting state of being that is not necessarily tied to a particular event or stimulus. The mood is often described using words like happy, sad, or irritable, lasting for hours or even days. It's influenced by a wide range of biological, psychological, and environmental factors. For example, it's been raining for a few days, so a person's mood could either be gloomy or "in-the-mood" for just sleeping or watching movies.

In conclusion, emotions are intense and short-lived responses to a specific event, while feelings are subjective interpretations of emotions that are often less intense and longer-lasting. Mood, on the other hand, is a more general and long-lasting state of being that is not necessarily tied to a specific event or stimulus. Understanding the differences between these concepts can help us better manage our emotional experiences and build emotional intelligence.

What Affects Emotions?

Many elements can affect our emotions, including:

Biology: Our biology plays a significant role in our emotions. For example, hormones like cortisol and adrenaline can cause stress or anxiety, while endorphins and serotonin can produce feelings of happiness and ecstasy.

Environment: Our environment can also have an impact on our emotions. Factors like noise, lighting, and temperature can influence our emotions, as are social factors like our relationships with others and the level of social support we receive. For example, dark environments could induce a state of fear and dread, while bright areas generate feelings of calmness and optimism.

Thoughts and beliefs: Our thoughts and beliefs greatly affect our emotions. For example, negative thoughts or beliefs about ourselves or the world lead to feelings of sadness or hopelessness, while positive thoughts or beliefs can develop feelings of bliss and contentment.

Past experiences: Past experiences also have a profound impact on our emotions. Traumatic or negative experiences may lead to feelings that cause tendencies of mistrust and low self-esteem, while positive experiences can create a state of confidence and assurance.

Cultural and societal influences: Cultural and societal factors also have a role in our emotional state. Some cultures find an event depressing, while others find it happy, depending on the norms of their society. Differences in perspective and emotions can also be observed among families; a family could feel happy when their daughter is getting married, while another wouldn't feel the same sentiment, depending on the family's beliefs, experiences, and upbringing.

Activity 1: Identifying and Labeling Emotions

Before moving forward, here's an activity that will help you and your partner identify each other's emotions by describing your temperaments and determining their triggers.

By performing this activity, you will understand more about each other's emotions, what's causing them, and how you can manage them.

To get started, keep in mind that our temperament is made up of tendencies and feelings that are influenced by four factors or parameters:

- Genetic Inheritance
- Physical Attributes
- Life Experiences
- Environmental Conditions

To give this activity a try, get started with the temperament questionnaire. First, make sure that you and your partner are calm and answer the questions together.

1. Describe your temperament with three adjectives. Choose the ones that describe you best, for example, angry, joyful, anxious, etc.
2. Think of three adjectives that others would use to describe your temperament.
3. Among the adjectives used in the above questions, which do you think suit you best?
4. Among the adjectives that were used in the above questions, which do you think suits your partner best?
5. How does each of the temperaments affect you on a personal level?
6. What triggers each temperament?
7. Which of these factors do you want to change and why?

Reflect on both your and your partner's answers because they are important to ensure that you remain understanding and empathic with each other's triggers. By doing so, you are helping one another to regulate your emotions and build a healthier communication system in your relationship.

Emotional Intelligence

Emotional intelligence (EI) is the ability to understand and manage one's emotions and also to perceive and influence the emotions of others. It includes a range of skills like self-awareness, self-regulation, motivation, empathy, and social skills.

People with high emotional intelligence are generally better at managing their emotions, allowing them to build positive relationships with others and navigate complex social situations. They are also more likely to be successful in their personal and professional lives, as EI is increasingly recognized as an important factor in leadership and team performance.

Emotional Intelligence and Relationships

Emotional intelligence (EI) is extremely important in relationships. It allows us to communicate effectively, manage conflicts, and build deeper connections with our partners.

Without EI, several negative emotions can take hold of relationships, leading to breakups and fallouts. Here are some examples of the most common destructive ones:

Anger: Anger is a common negative emotion that can arise in relationships. It can be caused by various factors, including unmet expectations, perceived injustices, and feelings of frustration. It can manifest as a range of feelings, from irritation and annoyance to intense rage.

Anger is a normal part of the human experience, and it can even be beneficial in certain situations, such as when it motivates us to act to address a problem. However, it can also be problematic if it is not managed effectively. Uncontrolled anger can lead to destructive behaviors, relationship damage, and physical health harm. Chronic anger can also contribute to developing mental health problems, such as anxiety and depression.

Resentment: Resentment is a feeling of anger or bitterness that occurs when one feels unfairly treated, wronged, or hurt by another person. It can be a powerful emotion that can cause a great deal of pain and suffering if it is not addressed.

Resentment happens in many contexts, such as personal relationships, workplace, or societal and political contexts. It can be a response to a perceived injustice, such as feeling that one has been overlooked for a promotion or that someone has been given preferential treatment.

If left unchecked, resentment can fester and lead to negative consequences, such as emotional distress, increased stress levels, and even physical health problems. It can also damage relationships and make it difficult to build trust and connections with others.

Jealousy: Jealousy can be caused by a perceived threat to the relationship, such as a partner spending time with someone else or being attracted to someone else. It can lead to feelings of insecurity and mistrust. Without emotional management, it could be harmful to the relationship as it could cause sabotage and other destructive behaviors.

Contempt: Contempt is a strong negative emotion involving disgust, disrespect, and disdain towards a partner. It can be a sign of deeper relationship problems and can lead to relationship breakdown.

Sadness: Sadness takes place in relationships for multiple reasons, such as losing a loved one or feeling disconnected or unappreciated in the relationship. It's important to recognize and address feelings of sadness to prevent them from turning into depression or other mental health issues.

It's important to note that experiencing negative emotions in relationships is normal and is not always a sign of a problem. However, it's important to recognize and address negative emotions when they arise to prevent them from causing damage to the relationship. Effective communication, empathy, and a willingness to work through problems together can help to mitigate negative emotions in relationships.

Manifestation of Negative Emotions

Often, partners don't show each other that they are feeling negative emotions in the relationship. Because of this, their lack of emotional intelligence goes unchecked, and it will manifest in various ways:

Difficulty expressing emotions: Someone with low emotional intelligence may have difficulty recognizing and expressing their emotions, which can make it challenging to communicate their feelings, needs, and frustrations to their partner, leading to misunderstandings and unhappiness.

Lack of empathy: Emotional intelligence involves understanding and empathizing with others' emotions. Without empathy, they may struggle to put themselves in their partner's shoes and understand their perspective, which leads to more conflict, especially during arguments.

Inability to manage emotions: Without this ability, people cannot regulate their emotions, and they could come off as aggressive and apathetic during conflicts. The inability to manage one's emotions leads to outbursts which could cause pain and anxiety to their partners. In worst cases, this may even lead to trauma, leading to the untimely fallout of a relationship.

Difficulty with conflict resolution: Conflict is a normal part of any relationship, but it can be challenging to resolve conflicts effectively. Emotional intelligence makes it easier to find common ground and work toward a solution that works for both partners.

Overall, a lack of emotional intelligence can make it difficult to build and maintain healthy relationships. It can lead to miscommunication, misunderstandings, and conflicts, eroding the trust and intimacy essential to a successful relationship.

Why EI is Important in Relationships

Emotional intelligence helps people regulate their emotions to act and communicate properly, even in challenging situations. Through regulation, here are some ways that can assist couples in building a "Sound Relationship House":

Effective communication

Emotional intelligence helps us to communicate our thoughts and feelings clearly and respectfully. With its help, we are more able to express ourselves and understand our partner's perspective, which can lead to more productive conversations.

Conflict resolution

Relationships are not always smooth sailing, but emotional intelligence can help us navigate conflict healthily and constructively. Through EI techniques, we can listen to our partner's concerns and work together to find a solution that works for us.

Connection Building

Emotional intelligence allows us to understand and empathize with our partner's emotions, even if we don't feel the same way. It helps us build a deeper connection and show our partners that we care about their feelings.

Secure Relationships

Emotional intelligence can help us build trust in our relationships. When we can communicate effectively, resolve conflicts, and show empathy, our partner is more likely to trust us and feel secure in the relationship.

Overall, emotional intelligence is essential for building and maintaining healthy relationships. It helps us have a deeper bond, manage conflict, and build trust and intimacy with our partners.

Building Emotional Intelligence

Seeing how important EI is, people should learn how to build theirs through practice and effort. Here are some strategies that can help you improve your emotional intelligence:

Develop self-awareness

Self-awareness is the ability to recognize and understand your thoughts, emotions, and behaviors. It involves being introspective and reflective about yourself and being able to observe and evaluate your thoughts and actions from a third-person perspective. It is a critical component of emotional intelligence and is important for personal growth and development.

There are two main types of self-awareness: internal self-awareness and external self-awareness. Internal self-awareness involves understanding your values, beliefs, emotions, and motivations. External self-awareness involves understanding how others perceive you and your impact on them. Both types are important for building strong relationships, developing effective communication skills, and achieving success in personal and professional pursuits.

Here are some ways to improve your self-awareness ability:

Practice mindfulness

Mindfulness involves paying attention to the present moment without judgment. This concept focuses on facts rather than perspective. It can help you become more aware of your thoughts and feelings and how they influence your behavior.

Journaling

Writing down your thoughts and feelings in a journal can help you gain insights into your behavior and patterns. It can also help you process your emotions and experiences.

Seek feedback

Asking for feedback from people you trust and respect, such as friends, family members, or colleagues, can help you see how people perceive you. Try to listen to their perspectives and be open to constructive criticism.

Take personality tests

Personality tests, such as the Myers-Briggs Type Indicator (MBTI) or the Big Five Personality Traits, can help you gain a deeper understanding of your personality and tendencies.

Reflect on your past experiences

Reflect on your experiences and how they have shaped who you are today. This can help you identify patterns in your behavior and thought processes.

And by Identifying your values and beliefs, you get a better grasp on how they influence your thoughts and actions.

Practice empathy

Empathy is the ability to understand and share the feelings and experiences of others. It involves putting yourself in someone else's shoes and seeing the world from their perspective. Empathy is a key component of emotional intelligence and is important for building strong relationships, developing effective communication skills, and promoting social and emotional well-being.

There are three main types of empathy: cognitive, emotional, and compassionate. Cognitive empathy involves understanding someone else's perspective and emotions but not necessarily feeling them yourself. Emotional empathy involves not only understanding someone else's emotions but also feeling them yourself. Compassionate empathy takes it a step further by feeling empathy and taking action to help and support the person in need.

Here are some ways to practice empathy:

Listen actively

When someone is sharing their feelings or experiences with you, give them your full attention. Listen without interrupting or judging them; this will show your partner they have your full attention. With this, they feel respected, heard, and valued.

Try to understand their perspective

Put yourself in their shoes and try to see the situation from their point of view. Then, ask questions to clarify what they're saying to show that you're interested in understanding their perspective.

Show compassion

Show that you care about how they're feeling. Offer words of encouragement or support, or simply be there for them.

Practice non-judgment

Avoid making assumptions or judging the person based on their feelings or experiences. Instead, accept their perspective as valid and acknowledge their emotions without minimizing or dismissing them.

Use body language

Use your body language to show that you're engaged and paying attention. For example, maintain eye contact, nod your head, and use facial expressions to show you're listening and understanding.

Practice self-reflection

Examine your own biases, beliefs, and assumptions and how they may impact your ability to empathize. Practice self-awareness to understand yourself better and how you relate to others.

By practicing empathy, you can improve your relationships with others and create a more positive and compassionate world.

Improve communication skills

Improving your communication skills can help you become more effective in your personal and professional relationships. This can also help you build emotional intelligence because it allows you to convey your feelings properly while also understanding others' points of view. Here are some tips for improving your communication skills:

Be a good listener

Active listening is an essential component of effective communication. Listen attentively to what the other person is saying and respond accordingly.

Be clear and concise

Be clear and concise in your message. Avoid using jargon or technical language that the other person may not understand.

Use nonverbal communication

Nonverbal communication, such as body language and facial expressions, can convey a lot of information. Therefore, use appropriate nonverbal cues to enhance your message.

Practice, practice, practice

The more you practice your communication skills, the more confident and assured you will become. Look for opportunities to practice, such as in meetings or social situations.

Use feedback

Seek feedback from others on your communication skills. This can help you to identify areas for improvement and build your confidence.

Be mindful of your tone

The tone of your voice can convey a lot of information about your message. Thus, you must be mindful of your tone and adjust it to match the situation.

Be open-minded

Be open-minded and willing to consider different perspectives. This ability can help you to build stronger relationships and communicate more effectively.

Improving your communication skills takes time and effort, but the benefits are significant. By practicing active listening, using nonverbal communication, being empathetic, and seeking feedback, you can become a more effective communicator in all areas of your life.

Manage stress

High-stress levels can make it difficult to maintain emotional balance and can impair emotional intelligence. To help you alleviate stress and achieve balance, here are some tips to reduce your stress levels:

Practice relaxation techniques

Relaxation techniques such as deep breathing, meditation, or yoga can help you reduce stress and promote a sense of calm.

Exercise regularly

Regular exercise is a great way to manage stress. Exercise releases endorphins, which are natural mood boosters and can help you feel more energized and focused.

Get enough sleep

Sleep is essential for your physical and mental health. Aim for 7-8 hours of sleep per night, and establish a relaxing bedtime routine to help you wind down before bed.

Eat a healthy diet

A healthy diet can help you to manage stress by providing your body with the nutrients it needs to function properly. Avoid foods high in sugar or caffeine, which can exacerbate stress.

Connect with others

Social support is an important factor in managing stress. Connect with family and friends, or consider joining a support group.

Manage your time

Effective time management can help you reduce stress by allowing you to prioritize tasks and avoid feeling overwhelmed.

Seek professional help

If your stress is persistent or interferes with your daily life, consider seeking professional help. A mental health professional can help you identify strategies for managing stress and provide support as you work through it.

By incorporating these strategies into your daily routine, you can manage stress and promote a greater sense of well-being. And remember that managing stress is an ongoing process; it takes some trial and error to find the strategies that work best for you.

Learn to regulate emotions

Emotional regulation involves managing your emotions healthily and productively. To improve this, here are some techniques you can apply:

Identify your emotions

The first step in regulating your emotions is identifying your feelings. This can involve taking a moment to pause and reflect on your emotions before responding.

Develop healthy coping mechanisms

Healthy coping mechanisms, such as exercise, mindfulness, and social support, can help you to manage your emotions healthily.

Use cognitive reappraisal

Cognitive reappraisal involves reevaluating a situation in a more positive light. This can help you to regulate negative emotions by shifting your perspective and reducing the intensity of your emotions. Truly, it's all about the mindset.

Regulating your emotions takes time and effort, but the results are rewarding. By developing self-awareness, practicing empathy, improving communication skills, managing stress, and regulating emotions, you can become more emotionally intelligent and build stronger and healthier relationships with those around you.

Purpose of Emotional Intelligence in Relationships

Indeed, building emotional intelligence is important in relationships not only to experience the benefits but to witness its real purpose. By communicating properly, a couple can enjoy the emotions that a healthy relationship offers, which is the purpose of emotional intelligence. It helps partners put meaning into their experiences, make their relationship worth fighting for and make their lives worth living. Here are the emotions that should arise when two people are in a healthy relationship:

Love

Loving and feeling loved are two of the deepest connections between partners. These connections involve shared experiences, emotions, values, and a sense of mutual understanding and support. In addition, they lead to a sense of commitment or devotion to another person, which gives the willingness to work through challenges and support each other through difficult times.

Joy

Joy in relationships can be a deeply fulfilling and rewarding experience. You can create a strong and joyful bond with your partner by cultivating positivity, communicating openly, sharing experiences, showing affection, practicing forgiveness, and prioritizing your relationship.

Gratitude

Gratitude involves feelings of thankfulness and appreciation towards a partner. It can help strengthen the emotional bond between partners and foster feelings of mutual respect and affection.

Trust

Trust is a foundational element of any healthy and positive relationship. It is a positive emotion that arises from experiences of dependability and reliability and can lead to a deeper emotional connection. It involves a sense of security and confidence in a partner so one can feel safe and secure with their partner and creates a strong bond of connection and intimacy.

Contentment

Contentment involves feelings of satisfaction and happiness with the current state of the relationship. It can arise from emotional security and a lack of conflict or stress.

Excitement

Excitement is a positive emotion that stems from trying new things together, experiencing novel or thrilling activities, or taking risks in the relationship. Excitement helps keep the romance alive, which is important to maintain passion and intimacy in a relationship.

Activity 2: Regulating and Managing Emotions

Seeing how important EI is, it's vital to learn how to regulate and manage emotions to build a long-lasting relationship.

In this activity, you will help each other accept your emotions and gradually regulate them by sharing them. However, by burying down emotions, you are at risk of emotional outbursts, which could damage your relationship. Once that emotion is triggered, it could lead to disastrous conversations and behaviors, leading to self-sabotage and relationship fallout.

Accepting your emotions means acknowledging and allowing yourself to feel them without trying to suppress or deny them. It involves acknowledging that emotions are a natural and necessary part of the human experience and that experiencing a range of emotions is normal and healthy. And since intimacy is an important aspect of a relationship, make this an opportunity to learn more about each other's weaknesses so you can uplift each other more in the future.

To start, both partners should think of the most significant event where they felt like the victim. Then, take two to five minutes to dig deep, preferably the situation that put you in a precarious or embarrassing situation.

Allow 15 minutes or so for the first partner to share their experiences. In this activity, the listener must employ active listening, where they show their good intent by rephrasing and displaying the elements of active listening.

After discussing the first story, switch roles and have the other partner share his feelings, then discuss.

Then, answer the following questions:

What story did you think first when you were told to share a difficult experience with your loved one?

How did you feel when you shared your story with someone else?

How did you feel after being acknowledged and accepted by your partner?

How did it feel after you acknowledged that your emotions were normal?

Did this exercise help accept how certain experiences made you feel and that it is okay to feel a certain way after negative experiences?

Did you feel more at peace after accepting the emotions generated by your experience?

Would you consider using this exercise to evaluate and acknowledge your emotions after negative experiences?

Perform this activity as often as you can with your partner, as it will help both of you to understand and acknowledge your emotions and regulate them before they bubble up and cause an outburst. You can also use this activity whenever you are arguing, so both of you get to have an equal opportunity to share how you feel and be validated by your partner. This way, you can create sustainable solutions without causing more conflict and fallout.

Signs of Emotional Intelligence in a Relationship

For some people, it may seem that having poor emotional intelligence is the end of the relationship. However, this is not necessarily true, especially when your partner is willing to work on improving themselves to make the relationship work.

By performing the activities above and learning about yourself and your partner's temperaments, hidden emotional trauma, and triggers, you are one step closer to being emotionally stable in your relationship. By understanding more about your emotions, you can communicate properly, listen actively, show empathy, and prevent sudden emotional outbursts. You may also observe these five indicators that you and your partner are getting emotionally stable in your relationship:

You start to practice self-love

When you start acknowledging your emotions, you don't feel as bad about your experiences, no matter how horrible they are. You start forgiving yourself, which is vital to your emotional and physical well-being. By understanding your emotions, you become gentler towards yourself and start appreciating your strengths and weaknesses. You don't beat yourself up about every mistake because you acknowledge that errors are what make us human and it's a normal part of life.

You become more interested in your partner

When you practice the techniques for emotional intelligence, you start to become more interested in one another. Since you already practice wholesome communication, both of you are more likely to talk to one another about your dreams, problems, and needs, which is essential in building a "Sound Relationship House." You also start to open up more about who you are, which allows your partner to widen their love map. By getting to know you, they will know how to make you happy.

They can support themselves

People with high emotional intelligence are aware of their bodies and emotions, enabling them to tend to their needs. For instance, having low bodily and emotional awareness is demonstrated by sudden intense outbursts. An angry individual is unaware of their emotions; they allow them to continue and fester, leading to agitation with others. If both partners have a moderate level of self-awareness, each wouldn't be completely dependable on the other, leading to a loving and strong relationship.

They maintain clear limits

With emotional intelligence, you'll know when to set boundaries. You don't have to put up with your partner's negative behaviors because you can now communicate your thoughts properly. For example, say your partner has bad habits; now, you can confidently start a conversation about it without offending your partner. Instead, you will communicate clearly and effectively to set priorities and work together to eliminate negative behaviors.

In summary, emotional intelligence (EI) is the ability to recognize, understand, and manage one's own emotions, as well as the emotions of others. It is important in building and maintaining healthy relationships, allowing individuals to communicate effectively, empathize with others, and positively navigate conflicts.

Individuals with high emotional intelligence can understand and share the feelings of their loved ones, which can help build a sense of closeness and understanding in relationships. In addition, emotional intelligence can also help individuals manage conflicts healthily and positively. They can control their own emotions, understand the emotions of others, and work towards finding a mutually beneficial solution.

Lastly, emotional intelligence can help build trust in relationships, as individuals can maintain love, joy, gratitude, intimacy, and excitement. In doing so, partners remain in a sound relationship house. They will keep widening their love maps to understand each other deeply and build a solid relationship foundation that will last a lifetime.

WEEK 3: IDENTIFYING NEGATIVE INTERACTION PATTERNS

Understanding the Cycle of Negative Interactions

If you are in a serious relationship, you probably experience some negative interactions with your partner, which is completely normal since everyone has flaws and negative attitudes. But suppose these interactions become the main feature of your relationship. In that case, It's only a matter of time before you and your partner realize how exhausting and draining these negative patterns are. But don't worry, even if it's a pattern, you can break it, and when you do, you will find yourself in a healthier and more stable relationship. Think of it as a challenge that strengthens a couple and allows them to add more meaning to their lives.

Couples are frequently engaged in negative cycles that can be challenging to escape. They may want to talk about what went wrong but need to know how to start the topic. In many cases, couples don't even know what's wrong or what's causing unhealthy thoughts and behaviors. They cannot figure out the root cause; hence, they go into a loop of creating unsustainable solutions only to find themselves in the same situation over and over again.

The Root of Negative Interactions

Whether you live with someone or spend most of your time with them, they get to see you at your best and worst. They see when you're stressed, how worn out you are, how angry and down you feel. And how these emotions may negatively affect how you behave toward others, which may cause pain, frustration, and disappointment.

Whether your words or actions are subconscious or not, they mean a lot to your partner. At first, they would be patient with you, help you through the challenges, and understand where you're coming from. But there will be a time when your partner gets fed up and shows emotional outbursts, which would hurt you back. If this happens, you and your partner will not understand where these emotions are coming from. So you start getting into this unhealthy pattern of arguing and fighting, thinking it's okay to prolong the cycle. Little do you know that it's slowly degrading the quality of your relationship.

In this chapter, you will learn the nature of negative patterns and how to finally break them and build a more secure relationship with your partner.

Emotional Intelligence and Negative Interaction Patterns

As discussed in the previous chapter, every element of life requires emotional intelligence, often known as emotional quotient or "EQ." In fact, a growing number of researchers determined that EQ may be more crucial than IQ (intelligence quotient) in predicting overall success in life. People with lower EQ tend to get into longer negative interaction patterns, but they can break the cycle with the right guide.

Now, let's take a look at the common negative patterns people with lower EQ tend to get into:

They Must Always Be 'Right'

When someone always insists on being "right," it can signify different characteristics. Here are a couple of possibilities:

Insecurity: They may be insecure about their intelligence or abilities. By insisting that they're always correct, they try to convince themselves (and others) that they're smart and capable.

Anxiety: In some cases, a person's need to be "right" stems from anxiety. They may worry about the consequences of being wrong or making a mistake and feel a compulsion to always be correct to avoid negative outcomes.

Regardless of the underlying cause, always insisting on being "right" is problematic. It can create conflict in relationships and make it difficult to work collaboratively with others. It can also be a barrier to personal growth, as admitting one's mistakes and learning from them is an important part of self-improvement.

They aren't sensitive to the emotions of others

Lack of empathy can have various negative effects on both individuals and their relationships as a whole. Some of the most notable effects include:

Difficulty forming and maintaining relationships: When someone lacks empathy, they may struggle to understand the feelings and emotions of others, making it difficult to build and maintain relationships.

Increased likelihood of conflict: They may also be more likely to engage in behaviors that cause conflict and misunderstandings with others, leading to communication breakdown and, if it gets worse, fallout.

Decreased sense of personal well-being: People who lack empathy may also struggle with being isolated and disconnected from other people, which leads to feelings of loneliness, anxiety, and sadness which will affect their treatment of their partners.

Increased risk of unethical behavior: Without empathy, people are more likely to engage in unethical or immoral behaviors, as they may not fully consider the impact of their actions on others.

Lastly, people lacking empathy may not feel motivated to help others, leading to a lack of community engagement and a decreased sense of social responsibility

They Act inappropriately

Most of the time, individuals with poor EQ lack communication skills. They might also have trouble distinguishing between proper and improper timing when speaking.

For instance, they might make a joke soon after a tragic occurrence or say something offensive during a funeral. Then, they act as if you are being unduly sensitive if you respond to their inappropriate remark.

Understandably, they cannot interpret and correctly respond to the emotional tone and mood, given their trouble understanding the feelings of others.

Playing the victim

"Playing the victim" refers to portraying oneself as a victim to gain sympathy or attention or to avoid taking responsibility for one's actions. It is often used negatively to describe someone perceived as manipulating by claiming to be the victim.

This negative pattern can take many forms, from exaggerating or fabricating incidents to gain sympathy to using victimhood to excuse one's shortcomings or mistakes. It can also involve constantly seeking out situations where that person can be called a victim and using it as an excuse to manipulate others.

Playing the victim can have negative consequences for individuals and those around them. It prevents individuals from taking responsibility for their actions and working towards solutions. For example, a partner can no longer address a behavioral issue because they fear the other will gaslight them into thinking they're the one at fault.

Prone to Emotional Outbursts

One of the elements of emotional intelligence is the capacity to control emotions. Individuals with low EQ find it difficult to comprehend and manage their emotions. Without realizing what they are actually feeling, they resort to anger, irritability, and aggression, which affects their partners tremendously as they center discussions on themselves.

Narcissistic Tendencies

Those who lack emotional intelligence frequently dominate conversations. Even when they appear to be asking questions and paying close attention, they always manage to turn the conversation back to themselves. This is because they typically have to prove that their experiences are more important than yours.

Activity 1: How to Break Negative Behavioral Patterns

Seeing how detrimental it is to have negative behavioral patterns, it is important to break this cycle and restore the connection before things get worse.

In this activity, you and your partner will work together to break the negative pattern that you are in. By following the steps below, you can determine the triggers of the behavior, along with the feelings associated with them. Therefore, by understanding and acknowledging these behaviors, you and your partner can create a sustainable solution that would help you adjust to one another and achieve a sense of profound respect and contentment. Here are some steps to break negative behaviors:

Find the trigger first

Finding the trigger of negative behavior can be a complex process that involves understanding the context and the individual's thoughts, feelings, and actions. However, here are some general steps that may help you identify the trigger of negative behavior:

Observe the behavior: Start by observing the negative behavior in question. Try to be as objective as possible, and note the specific circumstances under which the behavior occurs.

Consider the context: Consider the situation in which the negative behavior occurs. Is there anything in the environment that may be triggering the behavior? For example, does the behavior only happen in specific places, around certain people, or in response to certain events?

Identify patterns: Look for patterns in the behavior. For example, does the behavior occur at certain times of the day or in response to specific triggers? Are there any commonalities in the situations where the behavior occurs?

Consider external factors: Think about any external factors that may be contributing to the behavior. For example, is the individual under a lot of pressure? Are they dealing with a difficult situation or life event?

Answer these questions together:

What caused you to feel that something was wrong? When did you start feeling more irritated and more aggressive toward your partner?

Understanding your portion of the cycle requires paying attention to the initiating event that caused the mental dissociation. After all, you and your partner should be aware of what you saw or heard that prompted your response. This initial incident in the chain of circumstances starts the negative cycle.

Remember that identifying the trigger of negative behavior is just the first step in the process. Once you have identified the trigger, you will need to work with the individual to develop strategies to address the behavior and help them respond differently in similar situations in the future.

Identify Your Physiological Reaction

In general, physiological reactions are bodily responses that occur in response to external or internal stimuli. These reactions can include changes in heart rate, blood pressure, breathing rate, muscle tension, and skin conductance.

Physiological reactions can be voluntary and involuntary, and various factors such as stress, anxiety, fear, excitement, and physical exertion can influence them. For example, if you are experiencing stress or anxiety, you may notice an increased heart rate, rapid breathing, and muscle tension. Likewise, you may experience increased heart rate, breathing rate, and sweating if you physically exert yourself.

Ignoring your reactions to stress is equivalent to dismissing the warning signs before the Titanic collided with the iceberg. Your body informs you that something is amiss because it doesn't feel right.

To identify your physiological reactions, you should pay attention to your bodily sensations and how they change in response to different stimuli. You can also use tools such as heart rate monitors, skin conductance sensors, or biofeedback devices to track your physiological responses objectively. If you have concerns about your physiological reactions or feel they are impacting your health or well-being, consulting with a healthcare provider may be helpful.

List Your Feelings

What emotion did you have as soon as the trigger occurred? Did you experience rage, sadness, guilt, fear, or hurt? A combination of several different emotions?

Unbelievably, merely the act of naming your feelings has the capacity to lessen their strength and enable others to comprehend how you were affected.

There is no need to rationalize, justify yourself, or defend your feelings. Simply try to name and describe what you felt. Regardless of whether they make cognitive sense or not, feelings are always real.

Be Aware of Your Meaning

Not everyone responds the same way to a particular word choice, emotion, or action as you do. Your past influences both the stimulation that can set off a negative cycle for you and the feelings and actions you do as a result. For this reason, it's crucial to consider how your interpretation of a particular conduct influences how you respond.

Here are some illustrations of creating meaning:

I believed that you despised me, that I was too much or inadequate for you, and that made me feel abandoned and rejected.

I got the impression that I had no influence or power.

I assumed you wanted to end our relationship because you made me feel lonely and unloved.

Your interpretation of a certain trigger occurs nearly immediately. To prevent yourself from assigning this significance to the situation as it is happening, it may seem difficult to slow down time.

It usually seems comparable to a place we learned to be sensitive to in the past, which is why it can feel so instinctive to interpret your partner's words or conduct.

For instance, a teenager with divorced parents might be sensitive to rejection signals. Survivors of trauma may become sensitive to messages about losing control. Our brains work overtime to keep us "safe" by constantly examining our surroundings and interactions for these messages due to these sensitivities.

Link Your Internal Reaction to Your Action

Sigmund Freud, the founder of psychoanalysis, developed a theory of defense mechanisms. According to Freud, these mechanisms are unconscious processes that help individuals avoid distressing thoughts or emotions. Here are some of Freud's most well-known defense mechanisms:

Repression

This is the most basic defense mechanism, which involves pushing distressing thoughts and feelings into the unconscious. However, repressed thoughts may still influence a person's behavior or cause psychological symptoms.

Denial

This mechanism involves refusing to acknowledge a reality that is too painful or threatening. Denial can be seen in situations like addiction, where the person may deny that they have a problem, despite evidence to the contrary.

Projection

This type of defense mechanism involves attributing one's own unacceptable thoughts or feelings to another person. For example, a person feeling guilty about cheating on their partner may accuse their partner of being unfaithful.

Rationalization

This involves creating a logical explanation or justification for behavior or feelings that may otherwise be unacceptable. For example, a student who failed a test might say, "the teacher didn't explain lessons well," rather than admitting that they didn't study the material.

Displacement

This next one involves redirecting an emotion or impulse from its original target to a safer, more acceptable target. For example, a person who is angry at their boss might come home and take out their frustration on their family.

Sublimation

This mechanism involves channeling unacceptable impulses or emotions into socially acceptable activities. For example, a person with aggressive tendencies might channel those feelings into playing a competitive sport or writing fiction.

To stop the negative cycle, you must be aware of the defense mechanisms you use. Then, once you observe that you're doing it again, you can control it and look for alternative ways to make yourself feel "safe." It's a terrific approach to get to know yourself better and let your partner get to know you better as well if you can link your behaviors to your inner world.

Talk to your partner about it

Next, share your triggers, physical response, emotions, and behavioral response with your partner to begin breaking the negative cycle as a team. You and your partner can begin to recognize the "warning signs" of your negative cycle if you communicate this knowledge about yourself in a non-defensive, non-blaming, and non-shaming manner.

Establishing emotionally mature romantic connections

We can experience the kind of love we dream of – one marked by intense intimacy, mutual compassion, genuine devotion, and soulful caring. But to achieve the pinnacle of romance, we need all the traits of a high EQ. This involves acceptance of having emotions that, if allowed to fester, could damage a relationship; and a watchful, active awareness to alert us to what is working and what isn't.

You can start dating before your EQ reaches its pinnacle, as falling in love is a catalyst for heart education. With two high EQs, you get a romance that never stops growing or loses thrill. Here are some tips to have a high EQ in relationships:

Tell your partner how you feel

Express what you feel whenever you are communicating with your partner. Open and honest conversations will make your partner feel closer than ever to you, strengthening your bond. There's no shame in showing your emotions because it makes you who you are and allows you to put meaning into your communication, making it more soulful and genuine.

Give your partner the love and support they require

Emotional support in a relationship is extremely important, especially during difficult situations where your partner feels stressed, angry, sad, or anxious. Showing up and doing what you can to ease their negative feelings can positively affect your relationship by reducing stress, anxiety, and fears.

These are some ways to help you give your partner the support they need:

Show appreciation: Express gratitude and appreciation for what they do for you and the relationship. This can be as simple as saying "thank you" for something they did or surprising them with a small gift.

Listen actively: Listen to your partner's words and try to understand their perspective. Ask questions and provide feedback and support, and be present in the moment.

Be there for them: Offer support at times of stress, sadness, or difficulty. Show empathy and be willing to help them through their problems.

Show affection: Physical touch, kind words, and thoughtful gestures can all help to strengthen the emotional bond between partners.

Respect their boundaries: Make sure to give your partner space when they need it and respect their boundaries.

Ask if you're unsure

If you're unsure about something in your relationship, it's always a good idea to ask your partner for clarification or to express your concerns. Communication is key in any healthy relationship, and being open and honest with your partner can help to prevent misunderstandings or hurt feelings.

When you ask your partner, try to approach the conversation in a non-judgmental and respectful manner. Use "I" statements to express your feelings and avoid blame or accusation. For example, instead of saying, "you're not spending enough time with me," you could say, "I feel like we haven't been spending as much time together lately, and I'm feeling a bit disconnected from you."

It's important to listen to your partner's response and try to understand their perspective as well. Then, try to find a solution or compromise that works for both of you.

Remember, it's normal to have questions or uncertainties in a relationship, and addressing them openly and honestly can help to strengthen the relationship in the long run.

Discover your partner

Learning more about your partner in a relationship is an important part of building intimacy and understanding. Here are some tips on how to get to know your partner better:

Ask open-ended questions: Instead of asking questions that can be answered with a simple "yes" or "no," ask open-ended questions that encourage your partner to share more about themselves. For example, "What was the best part of your day?" or "What are your goals for the future?"

Show genuine interest: When your partner shares something with you, show that you're genuinely interested in what they say. Ask follow-up questions, use open body language, and remember to be present.

Share your own experiences: Sharing your own experiences and thoughts can help your partner feel more comfortable opening up to you. Be willing to be vulnerable and share your feelings and thoughts.

Practice active listening: When your partner is talking, make an effort to listen actively and understand what they're saying. Avoid interrupting or planning your response while they're talking.

Remember, learning more about your partner is a process that takes time and effort. So be patient, open, and willing to put in the work to deepen your connection.

Be sensitive to traumatic experiences

When it comes to those we love in the present, emotional scars from the past should be considered. No matter how much you know about your partner, you can never comprehend their feelings if they have encountered trauma.

It's important to be sensitive to your partner's traumatic experiences in a relationship. Trauma can significantly impact a person's life, and it's important to be supportive and understanding.

Here are some tips for dealing with your partner if they have past traumas:

Be patient: Trauma can have a lasting impact on a person, and recovery can take time. So be patient with your partner and avoid pressuring them to "get over it" or "move on."

Listen actively: Listen to your partner when they share their experiences with you. Try to understand their perspective and avoid judging or dismissing their feelings.

Respect their boundaries: If your partner is not ready to talk about their trauma, respect their boundaries and give them space. Avoid pushing them to share before they're ready.

Be supportive: Let your partner know you're here for them and that you support them completely. Offer a listening ear, provide emotional support, and help them access resources or professional help if needed.

Educate yourself: Learn about trauma and its effects on mental health. This can help you understand your partner's experiences and be more supportive.

Make the Most of Change to Strengthen Your Relationship

Change can be a challenge in a relationship, but sometimes it's vital for relationship longevity. Here are some tips for making the most of change to strengthen your relationship:

Embrace change as an opportunity: Instead of seeing change as a negative, embrace it as an opportunity to grow and strengthen your relationship. This can help you approach the situation with a positive attitude and an open mind.

Communicate openly and honestly: Change can be stressful and lead to misunderstandings. To avoid this, make sure to communicate openly and honestly with your partner. Share your feelings, concerns, and hopes for the future.

Find common ground: Identify areas of agreement and shared values. This would help you work together to find solutions and navigate change more effectively.

Be supportive: Relationship changes can be difficult, and it's important to support each other through the process. Be a source of emotional support and encouragement for your partner.

Be flexible: Change requires flexibility and adaptability. Be willing to compromise and adjust your expectations as needed.

Focus on the positive: Change is challenging, but it brings new opportunities and experiences. Therefore, focus on the positive aspects of the change and look for ways to grow and learn together.

Remember, change is a natural part of life, and it's important to embrace it and use it as an opportunity to strengthen your relationship. By being open and supportive, you can navigate change together and become stronger on the other side.

SEE THE DIFFICULTIES YOU FACE AS OPPORTUNITIES RATHER THAN OBSTACLES

Seeing the difficulties you face as opportunities rather than obstacles can be a powerful way to shift your perspective and approach challenges more positively and productively. Here are some tips on how to achieve this:

Practice gratitude: Take time to appreciate what you have and what is going well in your life. Focusing on the positive can help you maintain a more optimistic outlook and better navigate difficulties.

Reframe the situation: Instead of viewing a difficulty as an obstacle, try to see it as an opportunity for growth and learning. Ask yourself what you can learn from the situation or how it might help you become a stronger and more resilient person.

Seek support: Difficulties can be more manageable when you have a support system. Reach out to friends, family, or a professional if you need help coping with a difficult situation.

Take action: Instead of feeling overwhelmed, take action to address the difficulty you're facing. Break the situation down into smaller, more manageable steps and take them one at a time.

Celebrate your progress: When you make progress in overcoming a difficulty, take time to celebrate your success. This can help you stay motivated and maintain a positive attitude.

Remember, seeing difficulties as opportunities takes practice and may take work. However, by adopting this mindset, you can build greater resilience, strengthen relationships, and approach challenges with greater confidence and optimism.

RESPECT EACH OTHER'S FEELINGS FOR ONE ANOTHER

Respecting each other's feelings is crucial to a healthy and successful relationship. Therefore, it is important to create a safe and supportive environment where both partners can express their feelings without fear of judgment or rejection. Here are some tips on how to respect each other's feelings:

Listen actively: When your partner shares their feelings, give them your full attention. Listen actively, show empathy, and avoid interrupting or dismissing their emotions.

Validate their feelings: Let your partner know their feelings are important and valid, even if you disagree. Avoid criticizing, belittling, or dismissing their emotions.

Communicate respectfully: When expressing your own feelings, do so in a respectful and non-judgmental way. Avoid blaming or attacking your partner; use "I" statements to express your thoughts and feelings.

Create a safe space: Make sure your partner feels safe and comfortable expressing their emotions with you. This means being open, non-judgmental, and respectful of their feelings.

Work together to find solutions: If there are disagreements or conflicts, work together to find solutions that work for both of you. Be willing to compromise and seek a win-win solution.

Remember, respecting each other's feelings is an ongoing process that requires open communication, empathy, and mutual support.

Maintain fun in your romantic relationship.

Maintaining the fun in a romantic relationship is essential for keeping the spark alive and ensuring that both partners remain engaged and interested in each other. Here are some tips for keeping the fun alive in your relationship:

Try new things together: Trying new activities, hobbies, or experiences can help keep things fresh and exciting. Whether it's taking a dance class, going on a road trip, or trying a new restaurant, try to explore new things together.

Play games: Playing games can be a fun way to connect with each other and create a lighthearted atmosphere. Whether it's a board game, video game, or card game, make time to have fun and laugh together.

Surprise each other: Surprises can be a great way to keep the romance alive and show your partner that you care. So whether it's a surprise date, a thoughtful gift, or a love note, take the time to surprise each other and keep things exciting.

Laugh together: Laughter is an important part of any relationship and can help create a positive, joyful atmosphere. Try to find humor in everyday situations and share a laugh with your partner.

Make time for each other: In the hustle and bustle of daily life, it's important to make time for each other. A weekly date night or a quick coffee break would do wonders for your relationship. It's vital to prioritize quality time with your partner.

Keep your relationship from losing its spark

There are five techniques to stop your relationship with your partner from going sour:

Give up blaming your spouse.

You need to own up to your involvement in a disagreement. Dr. John Gottman argues that discussing particular problems will yield greater results than criticizing your partner. A complaint might be, for instance, "I'm angry that you didn't notify me about spending money on new clothes. You know money is tight at the moment," "You never tell me the truth" wouldn't be the right response here; you need to acknowledge your role.

Practice settling disputes. Resentments should be addressed because they could ruin your partnership. Conflict will inevitably arise, and those who try to avoid it run the risk of close relationships. Dr. John Gottman advises against becoming defensive and disrespectful to your partner (rolling your eyes, ridiculing, name-calling, sarcasm, etc.). Instead of shutting down, have a good talk with your partner. Sometimes a brief interval is beneficial for couples.

Schedule sexual intimacy. Physical contact, according to doctors, produces oxytocin (the bonding hormone), which lessens pain and induces a relaxing effect. According to studies, it is also released during emotional touch and sexual orgasm. Physical affection also lowers cortisol levels daily by reducing stress chemicals.

Remind yourself of your partner's great traits. To foster affection and appreciation for your partner, Dr. Gottman advises that you look for areas of agreement rather than arguing vehemently for your position. Instead, consider their viewpoint and follow Gottman's five-to-one rule of interactions, which states that you need five positive interactions for every negative one.

Set reasonable expectations. Your dedication to your partner may suffer from the delusion that there is a "perfect person" or soul mate and that a happy relationship should be simple. Relationships are prone to ups and downs, and it's up to you to foster understanding and respect.

The truth is, even seemingly great matches have issues in their relationships. The important thing to remember is that resentment can be avoided by setting reasonable expectations and practicing damage control. By accepting responsibility for our acts and cultivating acceptance and compassion for our partner, we may best develop a relationship based on love, trust, and intimacy.

ACTIVITY 2: BUILDING HEALTHY COMMUNICATION PATTERNS

This activity is called the daily check-in for relationships. Daily check-ins are a great way for couples to stay connected and address any issues or concerns in their relationship before they become bigger problems. Here are the steps to a simple daily check-in activity that couples can try:

SET ASIDE A SPECIFIC TIME

First, choose a time each day when you and your partner can sit down and have a focused conversation without distractions. This could be in the morning, over breakfast, or in the evening, before bed.

START WITH GRATITUDE

Begin the conversation by sharing something you're grateful for. It could be something related to your partner, your relationship, or your life in general.

Check in on how you're both feeling

Ask each other how you're feeling and listen actively to each other's responses. This is a chance to share any concerns or challenges you're facing and express your positive emotions.

ADDRESS ANY ISSUES

If any specific issues or concerns need to be addressed, this is a good time to bring them up. Use "I" statements to express your feelings and avoid blaming or criticizing your partner.

END WITH APPRECIATION

End the conversation by expressing appreciation for each other and your relationship. It could be a simple "I love you" or a heartfelt expression of gratitude.

Repeat this process daily to build better communication with your partner and build your emotional quotient in your relationship. Remember, the key to a successful daily check-in is to create a safe and supportive environment where both partners feel comfortable expressing their feelings and concerns. By setting aside time each day to connect and communicate with each other, you can strengthen your relationship and build a deeper, more meaningful connection.

WEEK 4: ENHANCING EMOTIONAL CONNECTION

Emotional connection in relationships refers to the deep and meaningful bond that two people share. It involves a sense of mutual understanding, empathy, and trust that allows individuals to feel safe and secure with one another. An emotional connection can develop over time as individuals share their thoughts, feelings, and experiences.

In a romantic relationship, emotional connection is often seen as the foundation for a strong and healthy partnership. Both partners are more likely to feel satisfied and fulfilled when they are emotionally connected. They can communicate openly and honestly with one another and are better equipped to handle challenges and conflicts as they arise.

Emotional connection can also be important in other types of relationships, such as friendships, familial or professional relationships. In these contexts, emotional connection can foster a sense of support, understanding, and collaboration, leading to greater success and happiness.

Building and maintaining an emotional connection in relationships requires effort and attention. It involves being present and engaged in interactions, actively listening to the other person, and responding with empathy and understanding. It can also involve sharing vulnerabilities and being willing to be open and honest with one another, leading to more meaningful and fulfilling relationships.

Emotional Attunement

Emotional attunement is the ability to understand and empathize with the emotional states of others. It involves being able to accurately recognize and respond to the emotions that another person is experiencing. This can be done by paying close attention to a person's body language, tone of voice, facial expressions, and the words they use.

This concept is important in building and maintaining relationships, as it helps people feel seen, heard, and understood. When individuals are emotionally attuned to one another, they are better able to communicate effectively, resolve conflicts, and provide support during times of stress or difficulty.

Emotional attunement is often associated with emotional intelligence, which refers to the ability to identify and manage one's own emotions as well as the emotions of others. It is a skill that can be developed through practice and self-reflection, which can significantly benefit personal and professional relationships.

Lack of Emotional Attunement

When a person lacks emotional attunement, they are likely to feel detached from other people because of the inability to connect genuinely and wholeheartedly to others. As a result, they may come off as rude and insensitive to others, which will degrade the relationship quality over time.

Emotional detachment is a state in which a person lacks emotional connection or involvement with others or events. It can manifest as a lack of emotional response to things that normally elicit a response or a feeling of disconnection from one's emotions. Emotional detachment can be a coping mechanism people use to protect themselves from intense emotional pain or trauma.

Although being emotionally detached can be a choice because it could save people from feeling stress, detachment isn't always a choice for some people. Unfortunately, it can be a symptom of mental health conditions such as depression, anxiety, post-traumatic stress disorder (PTSD), or borderline personality disorder (BPD). It can also result from certain life experiences, such as a traumatic event, a difficult relationship, or a chronic stressor.

Signs of Emotional Distance

Individuals who are emotionally distant or withdrawn may show signs such as:

Difficulties establishing or sustaining relationships with others

Establishing and sustaining relationships can be difficult for a variety of reasons. Here are some common factors that can make it challenging:

Trust issues: If you have been hurt in past relationships or have had negative experiences with people in general, it can be hard to trust others. This can make opening up and building a strong connection with someone difficult.

Poor communication skills: Effective communication is essential for any relationship to thrive. If you struggle with communicating your thoughts and feelings, misunderstandings can arise, leading to conflicts and misunderstandings.

Different expectations: When two people come together, they bring their unique perspectives, values, and expectations. If those expectations are not aligned, it can lead to misunderstandings and disappointment.

Busy lifestyles: In today's fast-paced world, people often have busy schedules that make prioritizing their relationships challenging. This can lead to feelings of neglect and disconnection.

Personal insecurities: If you have personal insecurities, it can be hard to feel confident in your relationships. This can lead to self-sabotage and feelings of jealousy and possessiveness.

Lack of emotional intelligence: Emotional intelligence refers to recognizing and regulating your emotions and understanding and empathizing with others. Building and maintaining healthy relationships can be challenging if you lack emotional intelligence.

Past trauma: If you have experienced past trauma, such as abuse, neglect, or abandonment, it can make it difficult to form and maintain healthy relationships. These experiences can lead to issues with trust, attachment, and vulnerability.

If you are experiencing difficulty in establishing and sustaining relationships, it would be helpful to seek the support of a mental health professional. They can help you identify the underlying factors that are contributing to your challenges and develop strategies to overcome them.

Difficulties showing love or compassion

There are several reasons why someone may experience difficulties showing love or compassion towards others. Here are a few possibilities:

Lack of positive role models: If someone did not have positive role models growing up or if they did not receive love or compassion from those around them, they may struggle to show these emotions to others.

Attachment style: Attachment styles can be formed based on early childhood experiences and can impact how someone interacts with others in relationships. If someone has an avoidant attachment style, for example, they may have difficulty showing love or compassion towards others.

Building emotional attunement

Building emotional attunement can help improve communication, foster stronger relationships, and promote a greater sense of empathy and understanding. Here are some ways to build emotional attunement:

Validate their emotions

Validating someone's emotions means acknowledging and accepting the way they feel without judging or trying to change their feelings. When you validate someone's emotions, you communicate that their feelings are important, understandable, and acceptable.

Validation can help create a sense of safety, trust, and connection in a relationship. It allows the other person to feel seen and heard, which can be especially important in times of stress or emotional distress.

To validate someone's emotions, you can use statements like "I can see why you would feel that way" or "Understandably, you're feeling frustrated about this." You can also ask open-ended questions to help the person explore their emotions more deeply and offer support and empathy as they work through their feelings.

It's important to note that validating someone's emotions does not mean you have to agree with them or support any harmful behavior that may be associated with those emotions. Instead, it simply means acknowledging and accepting their feelings as valid and understandable.

Avoid judgment

Avoiding judgment during conversations is an important aspect of effective communication. When we judge someone during a conversation, we are imposing our own values, beliefs, and expectations on the other person, which can create a sense of defensiveness or conflict.

To avoid judgment during conversations, try to approach the conversation with an open mind and be willing to listen to the other person's point of view without immediately jumping to conclusions. It can also be helpful to ask questions to clarify what the other person is saying rather than making assumptions based on your perspective.

It's also important to be mindful of your own biases and judgments and to try to stay focused on the present moment rather than getting caught up in past experiences or future concerns. Practicing empathy, putting yourself in the other person's shoes, and reflecting on your own reactions and responses can also help reduce judgment and increase understanding and connection during conversations.

Find common ground

Finding common ground during conversations can help build understanding, foster cooperation, and create a sense of connection and trust between people. Here are some tips for finding common ground during conversations:

Look for shared interests: During the conversation, try to identify shared interests or goals. Even with different opinions or viewpoints, you can find common ground based on your shared values or interests.

Acknowledge differences: It's important to acknowledge and respect any differences that may exist between you and the other person. This helps create an atmosphere of mutual respect and open-mindedness.

Seek to understand: When you encounter differing opinions or viewpoints, understand why the other person holds that perspective. This can help you find common ground by identifying the underlying values or needs driving their viewpoint.

Brainstorm solutions: If you're discussing a problem or issue, brainstorm solutions that satisfy both of your needs. This can help build consensus and create shared ownership of the outcome.

Be present

Being fully present can help you feel more engaged, centered, and connected to your surroundings. Here are some tips for how to be fully present at the moment:

Put away distractions: When trying to be fully present, it's important to put away distractions like your phone or computer. Removing them lets you focus on the present moment and the people or activities around you.

Engage your senses: Engaging your senses is a great way to be fully present. Focus on the sights, sounds, smells, tastes, and physical sensations around you. For example, if you're on a walk, pay attention to the colors of the trees, birds chirping, and the feeling of the breeze on your skin.

Set intentions: Setting intentions for how you want to show up in a given moment or activity can help you be more fully present. For example, before a meeting or social event, take a few moments to set an intention for how you want to be present and engaged.

Practice gratitude: Practicing gratitude can help you stay focused on the present moment and appreciate the good things in your life. Take time to notice and appreciate the positive aspects of your current situation, whether it's a beautiful sunset or a conversation with a loved one.

Effects of Prolonged Emotional Distance

If a person continues to display signs of emotional distance, they may experience the following setbacks:

Strained relationships: Relationships with friends, family, and romantic partners may suffer if someone cannot show compassion. When someone consistently fails to offer support, empathy, or understanding, their loved ones may feel unheard, invalidated, or unsupported. This can lead to feelings of resentment, frustration, and disconnection in the relationship.

Social isolation

If someone is unable to show compassion, they may struggle to form close relationships with others, leading to social isolation. This can further exacerbate feelings of loneliness, stress, and anxiety and may contribute to developing mental health conditions such as depression.

Negative self-perception

The inability to show compassion can also have negative impacts on the individual themselves. For example, if someone consistently fails to show empathy or understanding towards others, they may begin to view themselves as cold, callous, or unfeeling. This negative self-perception can further contribute to feelings of isolation and negatively impact mental health.

Reduced sense of purpose

Compassion is important to a many people's sense of purpose and fulfillment in life. Without showing compassion, someone may struggle to find meaning or purpose in their relationships, work, or other aspects of life.

Coping with Detachment

Emotional detachment can be a challenging and distressing experience, making it difficult to form meaningful relationships and connect with others. However, there are several strategies you can use to eliminate emotional detachment:

Identify the cause

Try to identify what might be causing your emotional detachment. For example, is it related to a past trauma, a current relationship, or a mental health condition? Understanding the cause can help you find ways to address it.

Seek professional help

Consider seeking professional help from a therapist or counselor who can work with you to understand and address your emotional detachment.

Practice mindfulness

Mindfulness techniques, such as meditation or deep breathing, can help you become more aware of your emotions and physical sensations, which can help you become more connected with your feelings.

Engage in self-care

Take care of yourself by engaging in activities that bring you joy, such as exercise, hobbies, or spending time with loved ones.

Connect with others

Although emotional detachment can make it challenging to connect with others, building and maintaining relationships can be an important step in overcoming emotional detachment.

Writing

Keeping a journal can help you get your thoughts and emotions out instead of detaching from them. It may also help you notice patterns or triggers for your emotional detachment.

Avoid self-medicating with substances

While they may provide temporary relief, substances like alcohol can make symptoms worse or lead to more problems in the long run.

Getting a new perspective

Take some time to reflect on your beliefs and experiences and how they may shape your understanding of the situation. Consider if there are any biases or assumptions you may be making, and try to challenge these beliefs.

Remember, gaining a new perspective takes time and effort and may require stepping outside your comfort zone. But with practice, you can develop greater empathy and understanding for others, which can help improve your relationships and overall well-being.

Allowing Vulnerability

Allowing vulnerability is an important part of building and maintaining healthy relationships. Here are a few reasons why vulnerability is important and some tips for how to allow it:

Builds trust: Allowing yourself to be vulnerable with others can help build trust in your relationships. Sharing your feelings, experiences, and struggles with others can help them see you as more authentic and relatable, which can help deepen your connection with them.

Encourages intimacy: Vulnerability can also help foster intimacy in relationships. When you give yourself permission to be vulnerable, it can create a sense of closeness and emotional connection with others.

Helps with emotional regulation: Allowing vulnerability can also help with emotional regulation. Sharing your emotions with others can help you process and make sense of them, which can lead to greater emotional well-being.

Here are some tips for showing vulnerability:

Start small: It can be difficult to open up and be vulnerable with others, especially if you're not used to doing so. Start by sharing your thoughts or feelings on a less sensitive topic, and work your way to sharing more personal or emotional information.

Practice self-compassion: Being vulnerable can be scary, so it's important to practice self-compassion as you work on allowing vulnerability. Be gentle with yourself, and remember that it's okay to feel scared or uncomfortable when opening up to others.

Set boundaries: It's important to set boundaries when it comes to vulnerability. Decide what you're comfortable sharing and what you're not, and communicate these boundaries clearly to others.

Seek out safe spaces: Look for environments or people that feel safe and supportive when practicing vulnerability. This can be a trusted friend, family member, or mental health professional.

With patience and persistence, you can build stronger, more authentic relationships and improve your overall emotional well-being.

Attachment Bonds

Attachment bonds are emotional connections between individuals, typically between a child and caregivers, but they can also occur in adult relationships. These bonds are formed through interactions that involve the exchange of emotional signals, such as eye contact, touch, and verbal communication.

Attachment bonds in childhood are formed through a process called attachment theory. The theory proposes that the quality of the relationship between the caregiver and the child during the first few years of life shapes the child's ability to form healthy relationships later in life. Insecure attachment, such as avoidant or anxious attachment, can develop in children when their caregivers are inconsistent or unresponsive in meeting their emotional and physical needs.

In adulthood, they are also important and can affect an individual's ability to form healthy and secure relationships. Adults with secure attachment bonds tend to positively view themselves and others and feel comfortable with intimacy and closeness. In contrast, those with insecure attachment bonds may struggle with trust and intimacy and have difficulty forming healthy relationships.

Building and maintaining healthy attachment bonds requires open communication, trust, and mutual respect. It also involves recognizing and addressing any insecure attachment patterns and working to develop secure attachment through building positive experiences and interactions with others. Seeking help from a therapist or counselor can also be beneficial in addressing attachment issues and developing healthy relationships.

Effects of Insecure Attachment

Insecure attachment can have a range of effects on relationships, including:

Fear of rejection

The fear of rejection is a common human emotion that can be particularly difficult to deal with in relationships. It is the fear that others may not accept us, approve of us, or want to be with us, and it can cause us to avoid social situations or to hold back from expressing our true selves.

In relationships, the fear of rejection can manifest in various ways. For example, someone who fears rejection may hesitate to express their feelings and avoid conflict or confrontation or struggle with trust and intimacy. They may also be more likely to engage in behaviors aimed at gaining approval, such as people-pleasing or seeking validation from others.

Dealing with the fear of rejection in relationships can be challenging, but there are several strategies that can help. For example, practicing self-compassion and self-care can help build self-esteem and reduce the impact of rejection. It can also be helpful to build healthy relationships with people who accept and appreciate you for who you are, as this can help build a sense of security and reduce the impact of rejection.

It can also be helpful to challenge negative thought patterns and to practice self-affirmations, focusing on your positive attributes and strengths. Additionally, learning to communicate openly and assertively while respecting boundaries and needs can help build stronger, healthier relationships and reduce the impact of rejection.

Need for constant reassurance

The need for constant reassurance is common among people with insecure attachment styles. It arises from a lack of trust in one's partner and a deep-seated fear of abandonment or rejection. Those who need constant reassurance may feel anxious or uncomfortable when their partner is not around, and they may seek validation or attention to help alleviate these feelings.

While the need for reassurance can be understandable, it can also be exhausting for both the individual seeking reassurance and their partner. It can be difficult for a partner to constantly provide the reassurance needed, and the person seeking reassurance may become dependent on their partner for their sense of self-worth.

If you need constant reassurance in your relationship, exploring the underlying reasons for this need may be helpful. For example, are there past experiences or traumas that are contributing to your insecurity? Are there specific triggers that make you feel more anxious or vulnerable?

Once you have a better understanding of why you need reassurance, you can start to work on building greater trust and security in your relationship. This might involve communicating more openly with your partner about your needs and fears and working together to create a more supportive and nurturing relationship. In addition, focusing on building your self-esteem and self-worth through self-care, therapy, and other self-improvement activities can also be helpful.

Jealousy and possessiveness:

Individuals who experience these traits often feel anxious or insecure in their relationships and may worry that their partner will leave them or be unfaithful.

Jealousy is an emotion that arises when one perceives a threat to their relationship, such as a partner spending time with someone else or expressing interest in someone else. Possessiveness is a behavior that stems from jealousy, and it involves trying to control one's partner's actions, thoughts, or feelings.

While jealousy and possessiveness are common, they are damaging to a relationship. They can erode trust and cause partners to feel resentful or controlled. If left unchecked, these behaviors can lead to emotional or physical abuse and may ultimately lead to a relationship breakdown.

Fear of abandonment

This is a common emotion experienced by people with insecure attachment styles. It is the fear that those we care about will leave us, and it can arise from multiple factors, such as past traumas, childhood experiences, or difficult relationships.

The fear of abandonment can manifest in different ways. For example, individuals who fear abandonment tend to avoid getting too close to others or struggle with trust and intimacy. They may also become overly dependent on their partner or engage in behaviors aimed at keeping their partner close, such as being overly clingy or needy.

Tendency to isolate

Isolation is a state of being alone or disconnected from others. It can be voluntary, such as when someone chooses to spend time alone, or involuntary, such as when someone is forced to be alone due to external circumstances.

This can affect individuals depending on the duration and degree of isolation. Short-term isolation can be a healthy way to recharge and reflect, but prolonged isolation can lead to negative effects, such as loneliness, depression, and anxiety. Long-term isolation can also lead to physical health problems, such as weakened immune systems, and even increase the risk of premature death.

In the context of relationships, isolation can be particularly damaging. It can lead to feelings of loneliness and disconnection and can erode the bonds of trust and intimacy that are necessary for healthy relationships. Isolation can also be a warning sign of abusive relationships, as abusers may isolate their victims from friends and family to maintain control over them.

Unhealthy communication patterns:

Unhealthy communication patterns are damaging to the connection between individuals. Here are some examples of what unhealthy communication patterns look like:

Criticism: Criticizing your partner's character, rather than their behavior, can be hurtful and unproductive. It can make the other person feel attacked and defensive rather than open to talking.

Stonewalling: Stonewalling is when one partner shuts down and refuses to communicate. It can be a way of avoiding conflict, but it can also leave the other partner feeling dismissed or ignored.

Defensiveness: Becoming defensive in response to feedback or criticism can lead to a breakdown in communication. It can create a cycle of blame and counter-blame rather than fostering an environment of openness and understanding.

Contempt: Contempt involves a sense of superiority or disrespect towards one's partner. It can be expressed through sarcasm, name-calling, or insults. It's particularly damaging to relationships, as it erases feelings of love and affection.

Avoidance: Avoiding difficult conversations or ignoring important issues leads to a lack of resolution and fosters resentment over time. Addressing issues as they arise is important, rather than allowing them to fester.

If you recognize any of these patterns in your communication style, it's important to work on changing them. This might involve practicing active listening, being open to feedback, and avoiding blame and judgment. It can also be helpful to seek the support of a therapist or counselor who can help you identify and address these patterns in your relationships.

Perfectionism

Perfectionism in relationships can be a challenging trait to manage. People who struggle with perfectionism may hold themselves and their partners to very high standards, which can create a lot of pressure and stress in the relationship.

Perfectionism in relationships can manifest in several ways, such as:

Setting unrealistically high expectations for the relationship: Individuals with perfectionism have a rigid and idealized vision of how their relationship should be, which may not be realistic or achievable.

Being critical and judgmental: People who set unrealistic high standards are more inclined to be overly critical of themselves and others. This can create a negative and judgmental atmosphere in the relationship.

Difficulty expressing vulnerability: Perfectionists also struggle with showing vulnerability or imperfection in their relationship. This can make it hard for them to connect with their partner on an emotional level.

Fear of failure: They typically fear failure and may avoid taking risks in the relationship. This can lead to a lack of intimacy and growth in the relationship.

Feeling constantly dissatisfied: Perfectionists have a hard time feeling satisfied in their relationships, as they may always be looking for ways to improve or perfect the relationship.

To manage perfectionism in relationships, it can be helpful to work on building self-awareness and self-compassion. In addition, learning to accept imperfection and cultivating a growth mindset can also be beneficial.

Negative self-talk

Negative self-talk is a common pattern of negative thoughts and self-criticism that can have a negative impact on mental health and well-being. It takes many forms but typically involves a critical or judgmental inner voice focused on one's perceived flaws, mistakes, or shortcomings.

It can lower self-esteem and self-confidence, increase feelings of anxiety and depression, and lead to a cycle of negative thinking and self-fulfilling prophecies.

Here are some common examples of negative self-talk:

Catastrophizing: This involves assuming the worst-case scenario in any situation and assuming that everything will go wrong.

Personalizing: This means taking personal responsibility for negative events or situations, even if they are not within one's control.

Filtering: This entails focusing on the negative aspects of a situation while ignoring or minimizing the positive aspects.

All-or-nothing thinking: People with this mindset view things in black and white without recognizing the shades of gray in between.

Overgeneralizing: This involves taking a single negative event and using it as evidence that everything in life is negative.

To manage negative self-talk, practicing mindfulness and self-awareness and challenging negative thoughts with evidence-based reasoning can be helpful.

Building Secure Relationship Attachments

Seeing how detrimental insecure attachment is to a relationship, it's important to learn how to improve one's insecurity to build a more stable attachment.

Building a secure relationship attachment involves creating a strong and trusting bond with another person. Here are a few ways to build a secure relationship attachment:

Practice good communication

Good communication is essential for building healthy and positive relationships, both personal and professional. Effective communication involves a range of skills and practices that enable individuals to express themselves clearly and understand others' perspectives.

Here are some key elements of good communication:

Clarity: It involves expressing oneself clearly and concisely, using appropriate language for the context and audience.

Respect: It entails communicating in a way that is respectful of other's perspectives and feelings, even if there is disagreement or conflict.

Openness: Through being open and honest when communicating and sharing thoughts and feelings in a way that is constructive and non-judgmental, a relationship can bloom.

Empathy: Empathy involves understanding the other person's perspective and feelings and showing compassion and support.

To improve communication skills, practicing active listening, using "I" statements to express feelings, avoiding assumptions and stereotypes, and being aware of non-verbal cues such as body language and tone of voice can be helpful.

Spend quality time together

Quality time is a term used to describe the time spent with others that is meaningful, enjoyable, and productive. It is about spending time with loved ones in a focused, attentive, and intentional. Quality time can be valuable for building and maintaining positive relationships with family, friends, and romantic partners.

Respect boundaries

Respecting boundaries is important to building healthy and positive relationships with others. Boundaries are limits that individuals set to protect their physical, emotional, and psychological well-being. It is important to respect these boundaries to build trust and respect with others.

Here are some tips on how to show respect for people's boundaries:

Listen: Pay attention to what others say and how they feel. If someone expresses a boundary, take it seriously and don't try to persuade or coerce them to change it.

Ask for consent: Always ask for consent before doing something that may cross someone's boundaries, such as physical touch or sharing personal information.

Be open: Communicate openly and honestly with others about your own boundaries and respect their boundaries in return.

Don't assume: Don't assume that you know what someone's boundaries are, even if you have known them for a long time. Everyone has the right to set their boundaries, which may change over time.

Be flexible: Be willing to adjust your behavior to respect someone's boundaries, even if it is inconvenient or uncomfortable for you.

Respecting boundaries can help to build trust and respect in relationships and prevent misunderstandings and conflicts. In addition, it creates a safe and supportive environment in which individuals feel comfortable expressing themselves and pursuing their goals and interests.

Show physical affection

Physical affection is a way of expressing love, care, and connection with others through touch. It can take many forms, including hugging, kissing, holding hands, and cuddling. Physical affection is important for building and maintaining positive relationships with family, friends, and romantic partners.

Emotional Intimacy

Emotional intimacy refers to closeness and connection between two individuals in which they share their innermost thoughts, feelings, and experiences without fear of judgment or rejection. It involves feeling seen, heard, and understood by another person on a deep and meaningful level.

It is an important aspect of any close relationship, including romantic partnerships, friendships, and familial relationships. It helps build trust, foster open communication, and deepen the emotional bond between individuals. Emotional intimacy also allows individuals to feel supported, validated, and secure in their relationships.

To cultivate emotional intimacy, individuals need to be willing to be vulnerable and share their feelings and thoughts honestly and openly. They also need to be receptive to their partner's emotions and demonstrate empathy and active listening skills. Other ways to build emotional intimacy include engaging in shared activities, creating meaningful rituals or traditions, and finding opportunities to express gratitude and appreciation for each other.

Building Emotional Intimacy through Shared Experience

Building emotional intimacy can take time and effort, but it can be incredibly rewarding in fostering deeper connections and stronger relationships. One of the best ways to develop intimacy is through shared experience, which is participating in activities that both of you enjoy and making new memories.

Shared experiences are a powerful way to build intimacy in a relationship. When couples participate in activities together, they create memories and experiences that strengthen their emotional bond. Here are some ways that shared experiences can help build intimacy:

Increased emotional connection: Participating in activities together can help deepen your emotional connection with your partner as you share experiences, memories, and emotions.

Positive memories: Shared experiences can create positive memories that you can look back on and reminisce about, strengthening your bond.

Greater understanding: Sharing experiences with your partner can help you better understand their personality, interests, and values.

Team building: Shared experiences can create a sense of teamwork, which can benefit any relationship.

Sense of adventure: Trying new things with your partner can create a sense of adventure and excitement, which can be a fun way to build intimacy.

You could use many ways to build intimacy through sharing experiences with your significant other. It could be anything from hiking, cooking, traveling, or taking a class together. The key is to find activities that you both enjoy and that allow you to spend quality time together.

During the activity, try to be present and engage with each other. Take the time to listen to each other's thoughts and feelings about the experience, and try to understand how it impacted each of you. You can also take the opportunity to express your gratitude and appreciation for your partner and the shared experience.

Building intimacy through shared experiences is ultimately about creating positive memories and strengthening the emotional bond between partners. Sharing experiences can create a deeper connection with your partner and build a stronger, more fulfilling relationship.

Activity 1: Enhancing Emotional Connection

This activity is called "5 Things," in which you and your partner will sit with each other and discuss random topics that would pique your interest. To play five things, you must choose a topic or put several topics in a jar and pick one. Then, each partner should say five things about it.

- Five things that made me smile today.
- Five things I would like to try.
- Five things I would rather do.
- Five things I like about you.
- Five things I like to do around the house.

You can think of more topics to choose from as long as it's interesting to you and your partner. This will help both of you get to know each other as you discuss your answers. Answering questions like "What do you like to try?" could also help you foster shared experiences and make new memories.

Remember to employ good communication strategies during this activity, so you and your partner can enjoy it.

WEEK 5: RESOLVING CONFLICTS

Conflict resolution refers to the process of addressing and managing conflicts between individuals or groups in a peaceful and constructive manner. It involves identifying the underlying issues causing the conflict and finding a mutually acceptable solution that satisfies the needs and interests of both partners.

Benefits of Effective Conflict Resolution in Relationships

Applying effective conflict resolution techniques leads to improved relationships, and it shows in different ways, such as:

Increased trust:

When conflicts are resolved effectively, they increase trust between partners, which is vital to maintain secure relationships.

Enhanced empathy and understanding:

To resolve conflicts, individuals must understand each others' perspectives, which can lead to greater empathy and understanding between individuals or groups.

Better problem-solving skills:

When conflicts are resolved effectively, they help couples develop better problem-solving skills, improving relationships in many areas.

Greater respect:

Effective conflict resolution leads to greater respect between partners, enhancing relationships and promoting cooperation.

Reduced time spent on conflicts: Conflicts can be time-consuming, and by resolving them effectively, partners can free up time to focus on other tasks and goals. These goals may include anything that would improve the status of the relationship and their personal lives.

Improved teamwork: Effective conflict resolution means improved teamwork, which helps partners work more effectively together to achieve their goals and dreams.

Greater motivation: When conflicts are resolved effectively, it can lead to greater motivation and a more positive attitude towards work or other shared goals.

Better decision-making: Conflict resolution involves making decisions that benefit all parties involved, and these decision-making skills can be applied to other areas of work or life.

Creates a more positive environment: Effective conflict resolution can lead to a more positive and supportive environment, reducing stress levels and improving overall well-being.

Greater emotional stability: When conflicts are resolved effectively, couples can achieve greater emotional stability and well-being, reducing stress and creating more happiness and satisfaction.

In conclusion, effective conflict resolution leads to better relationship decision-making by promoting open communication, empathy, understanding, collaboration, and trust. In addition, by managing conflicts effectively, partners work together more effectively, leading to greater success in their personal and professional lives.

Lack of Effective Conflict Resolution in Relationships

Conflicts, if left unresolved, a relationship is likely to be filled with the following negative aspects:

Increased tension and stress: When conflicts are not resolved effectively, it leads to increased tension and stress in relationships, which can be observed in many forms, such as:

Avoidance: When conflicts are not addressed, it can create an atmosphere of avoidance, where partners choose to avoid interacting with each other, leading to a breakdown in communication and reduced harmony.

Emotional distress: Unresolved conflicts can cause emotional distress for those involved, leading to anger, frustration, and anxiety.

Misunderstandings: When conflicts are not resolved, misunderstandings can arise, leading to further tension and stress in relationships.

Physical symptoms: The stress resulting from accumulated conflicts leads to physical symptoms such as headaches, fatigue, and insomnia, further exacerbating stress levels.

Increased conflict: When conflicts are not resolved, it can lead to a cycle of escalating conflict, where each party becomes more defensive and aggressive in response to the other's behavior.

Communication breakdown

Understandably, conflicts and problems generally take their toll on relationships, and communication is one aspect that gets affected the most. Some negative effects involve:

Reduced willingness to communicate: When conflicts are left unresolved, partners become hesitant to communicate with each other, fearing that the conflict will escalate or become more difficult to manage.

Increased defensiveness: When conflicts are not resolved, partners turn more defensive in their communication, making it harder for the other party to understand their perspective.

Lack of clarity: When avoiding conflicts, it can be difficult to establish clear expectations or goals, leading to confusion and further communication breakdowns.

Unwillingness to compromise: Individuals may become entrenched in their positions, unwilling to compromise or find common ground, further impeding communication.

Overall, communication breakdowns can lead to a deterioration in relationships, making it difficult for partners to solve their issues. Effective conflict resolution involves developing strong communication skills, including active listening, effective questioning, and empathetic communication, which can help prevent communication breakdowns and improve relationships.

Loss of trust

Trust is another key aspect that gets negatively affected because of conflicts. Here are some ways that unresolved conflicts can lead to a loss of trust:

Broken promises: When conflicts are not resolved, it can lead to broken promises, making it difficult for partners to trust each other in the future.

Lack of transparency: When partners may feel uncomfortable sharing information or being open with each other about their problems, it leads to a lack of transparency, which consecutively affects trust.

Perceived betrayal: Unresolved conflicts can also lead to perceived betrayals, where partners feel the other party has acted against their interests.

Negative emotions: Unresolved conflicts can lead to negative emotions such as anger, frustration, and resentment, further eroding trust between individuals or groups.

Reduced productivity

Unresolved conflicts in relationships can lead to reduced productivity. Here are some ways that conflicts can impact productivity:

Distractions: When conflicts arise, they can become a distraction, diverting attention away from tasks or goals and reducing overall productivity.

Missed opportunities: Conflicts can also lead to missed opportunities, where partners may fail to take advantage of opportunities due to disagreements or miscommunication.

Reduced motivation: Unresolved conflicts can lead to reduced motivation, where couples could lose interest or enthusiasm for tasks or goals.

Increased stress: Conflicts can lead to increased stress, further reducing productivity by impairing cognitive function and increasing absenteeism.

Increased turnover: Unresolved conflicts can lead to fallout, leading partners to leave the relationship due to dissatisfaction with the conflict resolution process or the inability to resolve conflicts effectively.

The impact of unresolved conflicts on productivity can be significant, highlighting the importance of developing effective conflict resolution strategies to maintain productivity and achieve goals. By managing conflicts effectively, couples can work together more effectively, increasing motivation, reducing stress, and achieving greater success.

Escalation of conflict

Unresolved conflicts in relationships can lead to an escalation, where the conflict becomes more intense and difficult to manage. Here are some ways that conflicts can escalate:

Increased emotions: Conflicts can lead to increased emotions such as anger, frustration, and resentment, further escalating the conflict.

Involvement of others: sometimes, the couple chooses to get other people to help with the problems, but with many people involved, it can escalate the conflict.

Negative impact on mental health

The lack of conflict resolution in relationships can negatively affect mental health. Here are some ways that it can impact mental health:

Reduced self-esteem: Individuals involved in unresolved conflicts may experience reduced self-esteem or self-worth, contributing to anxiety and depression.

Social isolation: Unresolved conflicts can lead to social isolation, where individuals may withdraw from relationships or avoid social situations, contributing to feelings of loneliness and depression.

Reduced quality of life: Unresolved conflicts can impact the overall quality of life, leading to decreased satisfaction and enjoyment in everyday activities.

Physical health issues: Chronic stress resulting from unresolved conflicts can lead to physical health issues such as heart disease, high blood pressure, and other conditions.

Increased stress and anxiety: Unresolved conflicts can lead to increased stress and anxiety, negatively impacting mental health.

Depression: Prolonged conflicts can also lead to depression, making it difficult for individuals to function effectively in their personal and professional lives.

The lack of conflict resolution in relationships can significantly negatively affect mental health. Conversely, effective conflict resolution strategies, such as communication skills, active listening, and empathy, can help to reduce stress and negative emotions, improve self-esteem and social connections, and enhance the overall quality of life.

Approaches to Conflict Resolution

Seeing how important conflict resolution is, it's time to delve into some of the most common approaches people need to know to solve a conflict effectively.

There are several approaches to conflict resolution, each with its strengths and weaknesses. Here are some of the most common approaches:

Collaborative approach

This approach involves working together to find a mutually agreeable solution. It focuses on open communication, active listening, and finding a solution that meets everyone's needs. This approach can be time-consuming but can lead to long-lasting, win-win solutions.

Compromising approach

This approach involves finding a middle ground that everyone can live with. It involves some give-and-take, and everyone must be willing to make concessions. This approach can be effective for conflicts where both parties have equally important goals or when time is of the essence.

Accommodating approach

This approach involves putting the other party's needs and goals ahead of one's own. This can be an effective approach when the relationship between the parties is more important than the issue at hand.

Competing approach

This approach involves winning at all costs. It can be effective when one party needs to assert its dominance or when time is of the essence. However, this approach can lead to long-term damage to relationships and create a charged atmosphere, with one partner being the "winner" and the other the "loser.".

Avoiding approach

This approach entails avoiding the conflict altogether. It can be effective when the issue is minor or when emotions are high. However, it can also lead to resentment and can prevent the parties from finding a mutually agreeable solution.

The most effective approach to conflict resolution will depend on the specific situation and the couples' goals. You may need a combination of approaches to find a solution that works for everyone.

The Conflict Resolution Process

Now that you know the different approaches you can use to resolve conflicts, you should know by now the approach you need to use to fix things with your partner. The chosen approach will be your basis in employing the conflict resolution process, as it will help you identify your goals and the best solutions for your partnership.

The conflict resolution process involves several steps, which may vary depending on the nature of the conflict and both parties involved. Here are some common steps in the conflict resolution process:

Identify the conflict

The first step is to identify the issue or issues causing the conflict. This involves talking to one's partner, gathering information, and analyzing the situation.

These are some ways to identify conflicts in a relationship:

Notice changes in behavior: Changes such as increased tension, frequent arguments, or withdrawal can be signs of underlying conflicts in the relationship.

Identify patterns: If conflicts tend to occur in specific situations or around particular topics, this can be a sign of a hidden conflict.

Listen for complaints or criticisms: Complaints or criticisms from one or both parties can indicate underlying conflicts. These complaints or criticisms may be specific or general and can involve anything from household chores to communication problems.

Pay attention to body language: Nonverbal cues such as eye rolling, crossed arms, or tense facial expressions signify repressed conflicts.

Be aware of avoidance: Avoiding difficult conversations or withdrawing from the relationship implies latent conflicts.

Notice changes in intimacy: Changes in physical intimacy or emotional connection can reflect underlying conflicts.

By being aware of these signs and paying attention to changes in behavior, communication, and intimacy, individuals can identify conflicts in their relationships and take steps to resolve them effectively. It's important to approach conflicts with an open mind and a willingness to listen and understand the other party's perspective. Effective conflict resolution can lead to stronger, more fulfilling relationships based on mutual respect and cooperation.

Listen and communicate

Effective communication is critical to resolving conflicts. Each party should be able to express their concerns and perspectives without judgment. Active listening, paraphrasing, and asking clarifying questions help ensure everyone understands the issues and each other's positions.

Here are some steps to follow when communicating about a conflict:

Choose the right time and place: It's important to choose a time and place where both parties can communicate without interruption and with minimal distractions.

Use "I" statements: When communicating about a conflict, use "I" statements to express your feelings and concerns rather than blaming the other person.

Listen actively: Active listening involves giving the other person your full attention, asking questions to clarify their perspective, and reflecting on what you hear to ensure you understand their point of view.

Avoid interrupting: Interrupting can be frustrating and prevent effective communication. Instead, allow the other person to finish speaking before responding.

Identify common ground

Once everyone has had the opportunity to share their perspective, it's important to identify any common ground or shared interests that can form the basis for a resolution.

Here are some ways to identify common ground:

Identify shared goals: Look for shared goals or interests that both parties want to achieve. Focusing on shared goals can help both parties work together to find a mutually beneficial solution.

Acknowledge the other person's perspective: Even if you disagree with the other person's perspective, acknowledging their point of view can help you find common ground. For example, you can say things like, "I understand why you feel that way" or "I can see why you might think that."

Look for areas of agreement: Look for areas where both parties agree, even on a small detail. Agreeing on something can help build momentum toward a resolution.

Focus on needs and interests: Look for each party's underlying needs and interests. Focusing on needs and interests rather than specific solutions can help identify common ground.

Take a break: Sometimes, taking a break can help both parties cool down and gain perspective. It also allows both parties to think about the common ground they've identified and how to move forward.

Both parties can work together to find a mutually beneficial solution by identifying common ground. It's important to approach the conversation with an open mind and a willingness to listen and understand the other person's perspective. Individuals can resolve conflicts effectively and build stronger, more fulfilling relationships by focusing on common ground and shared goals.

Brainstorm solutions

Brainstorming solutions can be an effective way to develop creative and mutually beneficial solutions to a conflict. Here are some steps to follow when brainstorming solutions:

Set ground rules: Establish some ground rules for the brainstorming session, such as encouraging all ideas, avoiding criticism or judgment, and building on the ideas of others.

Generate ideas: Encourage all participants to generate as many ideas as possible, no matter how unconventional or unrealistic they may seem. It can be helpful to write down all ideas on a whiteboard or paper to keep track of them.

Group and categorize ideas: Once all ideas have been generated, group and categorize them according to common themes or similarities. This can help identify potential solutions that can be combined or modified.

Evaluate ideas: Once the ideas have been grouped and categorized, evaluate each idea based on its potential effectiveness, feasibility, and practicality. Ask questions such as "How would this idea address the problem?" and "What are the potential drawbacks or challenges?"

These are some steps to follow when evaluating solutions:

Review the criteria: Identify the criteria established during the brainstorming phase, such as effectiveness, feasibility, and practicality. These criteria should be used to evaluate each solution.

Assess the pros and cons: Evaluate the pros and cons of each solution in terms of how well it addresses the problem, how feasible it is to implement, and what potential drawbacks or challenges it may present.

Consider the impact on all parties: Evaluate how each solution will impact all parties involved in the conflict, including their needs, interests, and perspectives. In addition, it's important to consider the potential consequences of each solution on each party and the relationship as a whole.

Rank the solutions: Rank each solution based on how well it meets the established criteria. This can help identify the best solution or combination of solutions.

Test the solutions: Test each solution by considering how it would work in practice. This may involve role-playing or scenario-building to evaluate how the solution would play out in real-life situations.

Choose the best solution: Based on the evaluation, choose the solution that is most likely to be effective, feasible, and practical. In addition, it may be helpful to choose a few solutions that can be combined or modified to create an optimal solution.

By evaluating solutions carefully, individuals can identify the best solution or combination of solutions to a conflict. It's important to consider the needs, interests, and perspectives of all parties involved and to choose a practical and feasible solution. Evaluating solutions can lead to more effective and satisfying outcomes and help build stronger, more fulfilling relationships.

IMPLEMENT THE SOLUTION

Implementing a solution is the first of the final steps in the conflict resolution process. Here are some steps to follow when implementing a solution:

Communicate the solution: Once the best solution has been identified, it's important to communicate it clearly to all parties involved. Explain the solution, how it will work, and what is expected of each party.

Get buy-in: It's important to get buy-in from all parties involved to ensure everyone is committed to implementing the solution. If someone is hesitant or resistant to the solution, take the time to listen to their concerns and try to address them.

Establish a timeline: Set a timeline for implementing the solution and establish milestones to track progress. This will help ensure everyone is on track and the solution is being implemented as intended.

Assign responsibilities: Assign specific responsibilities to each party involved in implementing the solution. Ensure that everyone knows what they are responsible for and is held accountable for their part of the solution.

By properly implementing the solution, individuals can ensure that the conflict is fully resolved and that relationships are restored. Effective implementation requires clear communication, buy-in from all parties involved, and careful monitoring to ensure the solution works as intended.

FOLLOW UP

Following up after implementing a solution is the final step in the conflict resolution process; it ensures that the solution is effective and prevents the conflict from reoccurring. Here are some steps to follow when following up after implementing the solution:

Check-in regularly: Schedule regular check-ins with one's partner to discuss how the solution is working and whether any adjustments need to be made.

Monitor progress: Keep track of progress toward the goals established during the conflict resolution process. Celebrate successes and address any challenges or setbacks as they arise.

Address any issues: If any issues or concerns arise, address them immediately to prevent them from becoming bigger issues. In addition, be open to feedback and suggestions for improvement.

Re-evaluate the solution: Periodically re-evaluate the solution to determine whether it is still effective and whether any adjustments need to be made. Then, be open to making changes as needed.

Express appreciation: Express appreciation to the other partner for their efforts in implementing the solution and for their commitment to resolving the conflict.

By following up after implementing the solution, individuals can ensure that the solution is effective and that the conflict is fully resolved. Regular check-ins and monitoring can help prevent the conflict from reoccurring

LEARNING EFFECTIVE COMMUNICATION SKILLS

Learning effective communication skills is important to make the problem-solving process more effective. Here are some techniques you can apply to communicate clearly and effectively with your partner.

ACTIVE LISTENING

Active listening is a communication technique that fully concentrates on and engages with the person speaking to understand and retain the information being conveyed. It involves giving the speaker your full attention, using nonverbal cues to indicate you are listening and responding in a way that demonstrates understanding.

Here are some key aspects of active listening:

Paying attention: Focus on the speaker and avoid distractions.

Demonstrating interest: Show interest through body language, such as nodding or making eye contact.

Asking questions: Ask questions to clarify or further understand what the speaker is saying.

Paraphrasing: Repeat what the speaker has said in your own words to demonstrate understanding.

Reflecting: Mirror the speaker's emotions or feelings to show empathy.

Avoiding interruptions: Allow the speaker to finish their thoughts before responding.

By using active listening skills, individuals can improve communication, build stronger relationships, and avoid misunderstandings or conflicts. It also leads to greater understanding and a more positive environment.

EMPATHY

Empathy is the ability to understand and share the feelings of another person. It involves putting yourself in someone else's shoes and trying to see the situation from their perspective. Empathy is an important skill for communication and building strong relationships with others. To improve empathy, you could try using these techniques:

Perspective-taking: Try to see the situation from the speaker's point of view.

Non-judgmental attitude: Avoid making judgments or assumptions about the speaker's feelings or actions.

Clarity

Clarity in communication refers to the ability to express thoughts and ideas clearly and concisely, without ambiguity or confusion. It involves choosing the right words, using appropriate tone and body language, and organizing information in a logical and easy-to-understand way. Clarity is important for effective communication and can help prevent misunderstandings or confusion.

Here are some key aspects of clarity:

Choosing the right words: Use simple and precise language that is easy to understand.

Avoiding jargon or technical terms: Use language that is familiar to the listener.

Checking for understanding: Ask your partner if they truly understand what you're saying.

By practicing clarity in communication, individuals can avoid confusion, prevent misunderstandings, and effectively convey their ideas and thoughts. Clarity can also lead to better decision-making, improved productivity, and stronger relationships.

Nonverbal communication

Nonverbal communication means using body language, gestures, facial expressions, tone of voice, and other nonverbal cues to convey meaning or emotions. It is an important aspect of communication and can complement or even override verbal communication.

Here are some key aspects of nonverbal communication:

Body language: Use of posture, gestures, eye contact, and facial expressions to communicate a message.

Tone of voice: Use of pitch, volume, and intonation to convey emotions and attitude.

Proximity: Use of physical distance to indicate social or emotional relationships.

Touch: Use of touch to communicate emotions or to show support.

Appearance: Use of clothing, hairstyles, and other physical attributes to communicate social status, personality, or emotions.

By being aware of nonverbal cues, individuals can better understand the emotions and intentions of others and can convey their own messages more effectively. Nonverbal communication can also help build trust and rapport in personal and professional relationships.

Respect

Respect in communication refers to respecting and admiring others, regardless of their background, opinions, or beliefs. It involves listening attentively, being open-minded, and treating others with dignity and kindness.

Here are some key aspects of respect in communication:

Listening: Paying attention to what others say and allowing them to express their opinions and ideas.

Being open-minded: Being willing to consider other perspectives and receptive to new ideas.

Treating others with dignity: Showing politeness, kindness, and courtesy towards others.

Avoiding judgment: Refraining from making assumptions or passing judgment on others.

Using appropriate language: Avoiding offensive or derogatory language and using respectful and appropriate language for the situation.

By practicing respectful communication, individuals can build stronger relationships, establish trust, and foster a positive and inclusive environment. It can also lead to better decision-making and collaboration, as individuals feel valued and supported.

Patience

Patience in communication refers to the ability to remain calm and composed, even in challenging or difficult situations. It involves taking the time to listen, understand, and respond in a thoughtful and considerate manner.

Here are some key aspects of patience in communication:

Delaying judgment: Refraining from jumping to conclusions or making assumptions before fully understanding the situation.

Clarifying misunderstandings: Asking questions and seeking clarification to ensure that everyone is on the same page.

Allowing for reflection: Taking time to reflect on the situation and the best course of action before responding.

By practicing patience in communication, individuals can avoid misunderstandings, build stronger relationships, and resolve conflicts more effectively. It can also help individuals remain calm and composed, even in challenging situations, leading to better decision-making and more positive outcomes.

Positive attitude

A positive attitude in communication refers to an optimistic and constructive mindset when interacting with others. It involves focusing on the good in people and situations, maintaining a can-do attitude, and reframing negative situations positively.

Here are some key aspects of a positive attitude in communication:

Being optimistic: Looking for the good in people and situations and expressing confidence in oneself and others.

Being constructive: Offering helpful feedback and suggestions and looking for solutions rather than dwelling on problems.

Reframing negative situations: Looking for the positive aspects of a situation, even if it seems negative at first.

Using positive language: Using uplifting, encouraging, and supportive language.

Celebrating successes: Acknowledging and celebrating the accomplishments of oneself and others.

By practicing a positive attitude in communication, individuals can create a more uplifting and motivating environment, build stronger relationships, and improve their well-being. It can also lead to increased productivity, better decision-making, and greater fulfillment and satisfaction.

By developing these communication skills, individuals can improve their relationships, resolve conflicts, and become better communicators overall.

Activity: Understanding and Resolving Conflicts

Before you end this chapter, it is important to practice resolving conflicts with your partner; start by playing a game called "Be the Fog."

This activity is created to help couples regulate their emotions when accepting criticism, as it is a normal part of life. Unfortunately, people fear opening up about their partner's errors to avoid conflict. Little do they know that conflict is a necessary step to achieve growth.

The game's goal is to have your partner tell you about your flaws or shortcomings, and you should absorb the criticism without throwing it back or responding in anger. Instead of getting mad or frustrated about the criticism, think of it as a way to improve yourself in the future. Talk about what your partner would want you to do instead, so you can both devise rational and attainable solutions to an existing problem.

However, before starting the activity, set some boundaries and try to have a safe word if criticism becomes too much. Overall try to be as respectful as possible and let your rationality take over so both of you can successfully go through the steps of effective conflict resolution.

WEEK 6: STRENGTHENING THE BOND

When you strengthen the bond in relationships, you increase the emotional connection and intimacy between you and your partner. This involves building trust, increasing communication, showing respect and appreciation for each other, and developing a deeper understanding of each other's needs, desires, and values. Strengthening the bond in relationships requires effort and commitment from both partners. It involves activities that enhance emotional intimacy, such as spending quality time together, sharing experiences, being vulnerable, and supporting each other through good and challenging times. Ultimately, strengthening the relationship bond leads to a deeper and more fulfilling partnership where both partners feel more connected and supported.

If you don't strengthen your bond in a relationship, it can weaken over time, and the emotional connection between you and your partner can deteriorate. This can result in a variety of negative outcomes, such as:

Communication breakdown: When the emotional bond between partners weakens, communication can become strained, leading to misunderstandings, conflicts, and a lack of trust.

Decreased intimacy: Intimacy in relationships is built on emotional connection, and if this connection weakens, intimacy can decrease, leading to less physical affection, emotional support, and sexual satisfaction.

Feelings of loneliness and isolation: Without a strong emotional connection, one or both partners may begin to feel alone, isolated, and unsupported in the relationship.

Decreased satisfaction: When the bond in a relationship weakens, satisfaction levels can decrease, leading to dissatisfaction, unhappiness, and even resentment.

Relationship breakdown: In extreme cases, a lack of effort to strengthen the bond in a relationship can lead to the breakdown of the relationship.

In short, failing to strengthen the bond in a relationship can lead to negative outcomes that can damage the relationship's quality and longevity. That's why it's essential to put in the effort and commitment to maintain and strengthen the bond in a relationship.

Benefits of Strengthening your Bond

Strengthening your bond with your partner has many benefits that can improve your relationship and overall well-being. For example, some of these benefits are:

Increased emotional intimacy: When you strengthen your bond, you increase emotional intimacy with your partner. This means you feel more connected and supported, which can lead to greater happiness and fulfillment in the relationship.

Improved communication: Strengthening your bond with your partner can improve communication, which is essential for a healthy relationship. Good communication helps to avoid misunderstandings and conflicts and promotes mutual understanding and respect.

Greater trust and security: When you strengthen your bond, you build greater trust and security in your relationship. This helps you feel more confident in your partner's love and commitment and can reduce anxiety and insecurity.

More fulfilling sex life: A stronger bond can lead to more fulfilling sex life. When you feel more connected to your partner, you are more likely to be comfortable with each other sexually and to enjoy a more satisfying and intimate experience.

Better conflict resolution: Strengthening your bond can improve conflict resolution skills. You will be more likely to listen to your partner's perspective and needs and to find solutions that work for both of you.

Increased overall happiness: Strengthening your bond can lead to increased overall happiness and life satisfaction. A healthy and supportive relationship can improve mental health, reduce stress, and provide a sense of purpose and fulfillment.

In summary, strengthening your bond with your partner can lead to greater emotional intimacy, improved communication, greater trust and security, a more fulfilling sex life, better conflict resolution, and increased happiness.

Building trust and commitment

Trust is a fundamental aspect of any romantic, familial, or platonic relationship. It refers to our belief or confidence in someone based on our experience and expectations. It involves relying on someone, to be honest, reliable, and consistent in their words and actions.

Trust

Trust can take time to build, and it is often based on a history of positive experiences with someone. When we trust someone, we feel comfortable being vulnerable with them, and we believe they will act in our best interest.

In relationships, trust is essential for building intimacy and connection. It allows us to be open and honest with our partners, creating a sense of safety and security in the relationship. Conversely, when trust is broken, it can be difficult to rebuild, and it can have a lasting impact on the relationship.

Building Trust

Here are 15 ways to help build trust in any kind of relationship:

Be honest: Honesty refers to being truthful and straightforward in one's words and actions. It involves telling the truth, even when difficult or uncomfortable, and avoiding deception, falsehoods, or misrepresentations.

Honesty is essential to healthy relationships, as it creates a foundation of trust, respect, and open communication. When we are honest with our partners, we build intimacy and connection, demonstrating our commitment to the relationship.

In addition to being truthful, honesty also involves being accountable for one's actions and taking responsibility for mistakes. It requires a willingness to admit when we are wrong and make amends when necessary.

Overall, honesty is a vital aspect of any healthy and fulfilling relationship. It allows us to build trust and respect with our partners and creates a safe and supportive environment for growth and development. By prioritizing honesty in our relationships, we can build strong and lasting connections based on mutual trust, respect, and understanding.

Keep your promises: Keeping your promises is an important part of building trust in relationships. Here are some tips on how to keep your promises:

Be realistic: Before making a promise, make sure it is something you can realistically deliver on.

Be specific: Make sure the promise is clear and specific so there is no confusion about what is expected.

Write it down: If the promise is important or complex, consider writing it down to help you remember and stay accountable.

Prioritize: Make your promise a priority and schedule it into your calendar or to-do list.

Communicate: If circumstances change and you cannot keep your promise, communicate with your partner as soon as possible to discuss alternative solutions.

Take action: Follow through on your promise and take action to ensure it is fulfilled.

Be consistent: Consistently keeping your promises builds trust and reliability over time.

Avoid overpromising: Avoid making promises you cannot keep, as this can erode trust and damage the relationship.

By taking these steps, you can prioritize keeping your promises and build trust in your relationships. Remember that keeping your promises requires effort and accountability, but the benefits of a strong and trusting relationship are worth it.

Apologize when you make a mistake: Apologizing when you make a mistake is an important aspect of building trust and repairing damaged relationships. Here are some tips on how to apologize effectively:

Take responsibility: Acknowledge your mistake and take responsibility for your actions. Avoid making excuses or blaming others.

Express remorse: Express genuine remorse for any harm or hurt caused by your actions.

Be specific: Be specific about what you are apologizing for and how you will make amends.

Listen: Listen to the other person's feelings and perspectives without becoming defensive or dismissive.

Avoid repeating the mistake: Commit to making changes to avoid repeating the same mistake in the future.

Follow through: If you promise to make amends or change your behavior, follow through on your commitment.

Be patient: Rebuilding trust takes time, so be patient and understanding as the other person processes their feelings.

Remember that a sincere apology can go a long way in repairing damaged relationships and building trust. By taking responsibility for your actions and expressing genuine remorse, you can demonstrate your commitment to the relationship and rebuild trust with your partner.

Respect boundaries: Respecting boundaries is important to healthy relationships and communication. Here are some tips on how to respect boundaries:

Listen actively: Pay attention to what the other person is saying and try to understand their point of view. This will help you respect their boundaries and avoid crossing them.

Ask for permission: Before you do something that might infringe on someone else's boundaries, ask for their permission. For example, if you want to borrow something of theirs, ask if it's okay first.

Communicate clearly: Be clear about your boundaries and communicate them to others. This will help them understand what you're comfortable with and what you're not.

Respect non-verbal cues: Pay attention to non-verbal cues, such as body language or tone of voice, to understand how someone feels. If someone seems uncomfortable, respect their boundaries and adjust your behavior accordingly.

Avoid pressure or manipulation: Avoid pressuring or manipulating someone into doing something they're uncomfortable with, which is a form of boundary violation.

Take responsibility: If you accidentally cross someone's boundary, take responsibility for your actions and apologize. This will help rebuild trust and show that you respect their boundaries.

Remember that respecting boundaries is an ongoing process that requires open communication, empathy, and mutual respect.

Be reliable: Reliability means being consistent and trustworthy in your actions and behavior. It means that people can count on you to follow through on your commitments, be there when needed, and do what you said you would. When you are reliable, people feel confident in your abilities and trust you to meet their expectations.

Being reliable requires a combination of qualities, such as:

Consistency: Consistently delivering on your commitments and promises is a key aspect of reliability.

Responsibility: Taking responsibility for your actions and being accountable for your mistakes is essential in building trust.

Punctuality: Being on time and respecting other people's schedules are important reliability aspects.

Communication: Being clear and open in your communication helps build trust and ensures everyone is on the same page.

Dependability: Being dependable means that people can count on you to be there when they need you, whether for work, personal support, or other commitments.

Overall, being reliable is an important trait that can help you build strong relationships, gain trust, and succeed in both personal and professional settings.

Show appreciation: Appreciating your partner means recognizing and valuing their positive qualities, actions, and contributions to your relationship. It involves expressing gratitude for what they bring to the relationship and acknowledging their efforts and accomplishments.

Here are some ways to show appreciation to your partner:

Say "thank you": Acknowledge and express gratitude for the little things your partner does, such as cooking dinner or taking out the trash.

Compliment them: Let your partner know what you admire about them, whether it's their sense of humor, kindness, or intelligence.

Show affection: Physical touches, like hugs and kisses, can communicate appreciation and reinforce your connection.

Do something special: Surprise your partner with a thoughtful gesture, like cooking their favorite meal or planning a special date.

Be supportive: Show your partner that you believe in them and their goals, and offer encouragement when they need it.

Recognize their contributions: Whether it's in the relationship or other areas of their life, acknowledge and appreciate your partner's hard work and accomplishments.

Appreciating your partner is an ongoing process that requires effort and intention. However, it can help strengthen your relationship, increase positivity, and deepen your connection.

Be consistent: Being consistent means being reliable, dependable, and predictable in your actions and behavior. It involves showing up consistently, following through on your commitments, and behaving consistently over time.

Here are some examples of what it means to be consistent:

Maintaining boundaries: Being consistent in maintaining your boundaries and values, and communicating them clearly to others, help you establish a clear sense of self and builds trust with others.

Behaving predictably: Consistently behaving predictably and reasonably over time helps others know what to expect from you and builds a sense of trust and security.

Communicating clearly: Consistently communicating honestly and respectfully builds trust and helps avoid misunderstandings or confusion.

Consistency requires effort and intention; it can help you build strong relationships, establish trust, and achieve your goals.

Be vulnerable: Being vulnerable means allowing yourself to be open, honest, and emotionally exposed to others, even when it involves risks or potential discomfort. Vulnerability involves sharing your thoughts, feelings, and experiences with others, even if it means being honest about your fears, doubts, or weaknesses.

Here are some examples of what it means to be vulnerable:

Sharing your feelings: Being vulnerable involves sharing your emotions with others, even if it means expressing difficult or uncomfortable feelings like sadness, fear, or anger.

Admitting mistakes: Being vulnerable means admitting when you are wrong or have made a mistake, even if it involves potential consequences or embarrassment.

Asking for help: Being vulnerable involves acknowledging when you need help or support from others and being willing to ask for it.

Taking risks: Being vulnerable means taking risks in relationships or other areas of life, even if it involves the possibility of rejection or failure.

Trusting others: Being vulnerable involves trusting others with your thoughts, feelings, and experiences, even if it means being vulnerable to judgment or criticism.

Being vulnerable can be uncomfortable or challenging, but it can also help deepen connections with others, build trust, and foster personal growth. It requires courage, self-awareness, and the willingness to take risks and be open to new experiences.

Demonstrate loyalty: Being loyal means being faithful, committed, and devoted to someone or something. It involves staying true to your commitments, promises, and values, even in challenging situations. In addition, loyalty involves a sense of dedication and devotion to others and a willingness to support them through thick and thin.

Here are some examples of what it means to be loyal:

Standing by someone: Being loyal means standing by someone's side, especially when facing challenges or difficult situations. It involves providing support, encouragement, and reassurance when they need it most.

Keeping your word: Being loyal means keeping your promises and commitments and following through on your responsibilities and obligations.

Honoring relationships: Being loyal means respecting the relationships you have with others, whether it's with family, friends, or romantic partners. It involves being faithful and committed to those relationships, even when it involves sacrifice or compromise.

Defending others: Being loyal means defending the people you care about, whether by standing up for them in a difficult situation or protecting them from harm.

Upholding values: Loyalty means upholding your values and principles, even in challenging or difficult situations.

Being loyal requires effort and commitment, and it can help strengthen relationships, build trust, and promote personal integrity. It involves a willingness to put the needs of others above your own and to stay true to your commitments and values, even when it involves sacrifice or difficulty.

Follow through on consequences: Following through on consequences means enforcing the consequences established as a result of someone's actions or behavior. It involves holding individuals accountable for their actions and ensuring that they understand the impact of their behavior.

Here are some examples of what it means to follow through on consequences:

Consistency: Following through on consequences means consistently enforcing the consequences every time the same behavior occurs. This consistency helps to establish clear boundaries and expectations and communicates that certain behaviors will not be tolerated.

Communication: Following through on consequences means clearly communicating the consequences in advance so that individuals understand the expectations and the consequences that will occur if those expectations are not met.

Clarity: Following through on consequences means being clear about the consequences and why they are being enforced so that individuals understand the connection between their behavior and the consequences.

Fairness: Following through on consequences means being fair and impartial in enforcing the consequences without showing favoritism or discrimination.

Consequences that fit the behavior: Following through on consequences means ensuring that the consequences are appropriate and proportional to the behavior that occurred. The consequences mustn't be too severe or too lenient.

Following through on consequences helps individuals understand the impact of their behavior and encourages them to take responsibility for their actions. It also helps establish clear boundaries and expectations and promotes a sense of accountability and respect for others.

By consistently demonstrating these behaviors, you can build trust in your relationship and create a strong foundation for a healthy and fulfilling connection. Building and maintaining trust can create strong, lasting relationships based on mutual respect, understanding, and support.

Commitment

Commitment is dedicating oneself to a person, cause, or goal with a sense of purpose, responsibility, and accountability. It involves making a promise or pledge to uphold one's responsibilities and obligations and to do so with conviction and determination.

Committing means being willing to go the extra mile to achieve a goal and staying focused and motivated even when facing obstacles or setbacks. It involves a willingness to sacrifice personal interests or desires for the greater good and to make decisions based on what is best for the person, cause, or goal being committed to.

Here are some examples of what it means to commit:

Determination: Having commitment means being determined to achieve a goal and to do so with perseverance and resilience. It involves a willingness to work hard, overcome challenges, and stay focused on the result.

Responsibility: Committing to someone means taking responsibility for one's actions and decisions and their impact on others. It entails being accountable for one's behavior and doing what is necessary to uphold one's responsibilities and obligations.

Sacrifice: Another important aspect of being committed is sacrifice, as in sacrificing personal interests or desires for the greater good. It involves putting the needs of others or the goal above one's own needs and making decisions based on what is best for the person, cause, or goal being committed to.

Consistency: Committing means being consistent in one's actions and behavior. It involves showing up consistently, following through on commitments, and behaving consistently over time.

Passion: Last but not least, commitment means having a strong sense of passion and purpose for the person, cause, or goal being committed to. It involves a sense of enthusiasm and dedication and a willingness to invest time, energy, and resources to achieve the desired outcome.

Committing requires effort and dedication, and it can lead to personal growth, success, and fulfillment. It involves setting clear goals and objectives and developing a plan of action to achieve them. It also involves staying focused and motivated and overcoming obstacles and setbacks along the way.

Building Commitment

Here are some ways to develop and maintain a strong sense of commitment:

Set clear goals: Committing requires setting clear goals and objectives that are achievable and measurable. This helps to provide a sense of direction and purpose and allows one to stay focused and motivated.

Develop a plan of action: Commitment involves developing a plan of action to achieve the desired outcome. This plan should include specific actions and milestones and should be reviewed and revised regularly as needed.

Stay focused and motivated: Being committed requires staying focused and motivated, even when facing obstacles or setbacks. In addition, it involves staying optimistic and seeking support and encouragement from others when needed.

Take responsibility: Committing means taking responsibility for one's actions and decisions and their impact on others. It involves being accountable for one's behavior and doing what is necessary to uphold one's responsibilities and obligations.

In conclusion, committing means dedicating oneself to a person, cause, or goal with a sense of purpose, responsibility, and accountability. It involves making a promise or pledge to uphold one's responsibilities and obligations and to do so with conviction and determination. Commitment requires effort and dedication, and it can lead to personal growth, success, and fulfillment. It involves setting clear goals and objectives, developing a plan of action, staying focused and motivated, taking responsibility, and staying consistent in one's actions and behavior over time.

Developing a Shared Vision for the Future

Developing a shared vision for the future in a relationship is an important process that can help couples to align their goals and aspirations and create a shared sense of purpose and direction. A shared vision is a powerful tool for building a strong and fulfilling relationship and can provide a sense of motivation and commitment to achieving common goals.

Here are some key steps in developing a shared vision for the future in a relationship:

Start with open and honest communication: Developing a shared vision for the future in a relationship requires open and honest communication. Couples should set aside time to discuss their individual goals and aspirations and explore ways in which they can support each other in achieving those goals. It's important to listen actively and empathetically and to be open to new ideas and perspectives.

Identify common values and interests: To create a shared vision, couples must identify their common values and interests. This involves exploring the important things to each partner and finding areas of overlap and agreement. Identifying common values and interests can help create a sense of alignment and connection and provide a foundation for the shared vision.

Set shared goals and objectives: Once common values and interests have been identified, couples can begin to set shared goals and objectives. These goals should be specific, measurable, achievable, and aligned with the common values and interests identified earlier. Setting shared goals and objectives can help create a sense of purpose and direction and provide a clear roadmap for achieving the shared vision.

Create a plan of action: With shared goals and objectives in place, couples can begin to create a plan of action for achieving their shared vision. This plan should outline the steps that need to be taken to achieve the shared goals and should identify any obstacles or challenges that may need to be overcome. Creating a plan of action helps ensure that both partners are on the same page and helps to create a sense of accountability and responsibility.

Review and revise the shared vision regularly: Developing a shared vision for the future is an ongoing process, and couples should review and revise their vision regularly. This can help ensure that the shared vision remains relevant and achievable and help to identify any areas where adjustments may need to be made. Regular review and revision can also maintain momentum and progress toward the shared vision.

In addition to these key steps, several other factors can contribute to the success of developing a shared vision for the future in a relationship. These include:

Mutual respect: Developing a shared vision requires mutual respect and understanding. Couples should respect each other's opinions and ideas and be willing to compromise and find common ground.

Patience and flexibility: Developing a shared vision can take time, and couples should be patient and flexible throughout the process. It's important to be open to new ideas and perspectives and willing to adjust the shared vision as needed.

Celebration and acknowledgment: As couples work towards achieving their shared vision, it's important to celebrate and acknowledge their progress along the way. This can help maintain a sense of motivation and create a positive and supportive atmosphere.

In conclusion, developing a shared vision for the future in a relationship is an important process that can help couples to align their goals and aspirations and to create a shared sense of purpose and direction. It requires open and honest communication, identifying common values and interests, setting shared goals and objectives, creating a plan of action, and regular review and revision. With patience, flexibility, mutual respect, and celebration and acknowledgment, couples can develop a shared vision that supports a strong and fulfilling relationship.

Re-establishing Your Love

Reestablishing love and bonding between couples is a process of repairing and strengthening the emotional connection between two individuals in a romantic relationship. This process involves a deliberate and intentional effort by both partners to overcome the challenges that have caused their relationship's breakdown and rebuild trust, respect, and affection.

The reasons for reestablishing love and bond can vary. Still, it's usually prompted by dissatisfaction, disconnection, or distance that has developed in the relationship. This could be due to various factors such as infidelity, communication breakdown, loss of intimacy, or external stressors such as work or family pressures. Whatever the cause, reestablishing love and bond requires a commitment to work together to overcome challenges and create a healthier and more fulfilling relationship.

The first step in reestablishing love and bond between couples is to acknowledge the problems that have caused the breakdown in the relationship. This requires honest communication between partners, where each person feels safe and heard to express their feelings and concerns. Both partners must take responsibility for their actions and avoid blaming or criticizing the other person. This can be a difficult and emotionally charged process, but it is necessary to address the underlying issues and begin the process of rebuilding trust and connection.

Once the issues have been acknowledged, the next step involves seeking counseling or therapy to work through underlying emotional issues or learning new communication skills to improve interactions. It may involve changing behaviors or habits that have contributed to the breakdown of the relationship. This could include prioritizing quality time together, being attentive to each other's needs, or making efforts to reconnect.

Reestablishing love and bond between couples also requires a willingness to forgive and let go of past hurts and resentments. This can be a challenging aspect of the process, as it requires both partners to let go of their pride and ego and focus on the relationship's future rather than dwelling on the past. Forgiveness is not about forgetting or excusing hurtful behavior, but rather it is about acknowledging the pain that has been caused and choosing to move forward with love and compassion.

Another important aspect of reestablishing love and bond between couples is cultivating a culture of appreciation and gratitude in the relationship. This involves recognizing and expressing gratitude for the relationship's positive aspects and for each partner's efforts to improve the relationship. It is easy to take each other for granted in long-term relationships, and focusing on gratitude can help to create a more positive and loving environment.

Finally, reestablishing love and bond between couples requires a long-term commitment to the relationship. It is not a one-time event or a quick fix but rather an ongoing process of growth and development. It requires a willingness to be patient, work through challenges, and invest time and effort into the relationship. It also requires a commitment to open communication, where partners feel safe and heard.

In conclusion, reestablishing love and bond between couples is a process that requires commitment, patience, and effort. It involves acknowledging the issues that have caused the breakdown in the relationship, working on addressing them, forgiving past hurts, cultivating appreciation and gratitude, and committing to the long-term growth and development of the relationship. It is a challenging process that leads to a deeper and more fulfilling relationship for both partners.

Activity: Strengthening the Bond

Now that you know how important it is to strengthen your bond with your partner, you need to figure out some ways to achieve this. There are many activities that couples can engage in to strengthen their bond and deepen their connection. Here are some ideas to consider:

Take a trip together: Traveling to a new place can be a great way to bond with your partner. It allows you to share new experiences and create memories together. Consider going somewhere you both have always wanted to visit or try a new type of traveling, such as backpacking or camping.

Exercise together: Engaging in physical activity with your partner can be a fun way to strengthen your bond while improving your health. Try taking a fitness class together, running, or taking a yoga class. Not only will you feel good physically, but you'll also feel good emotionally as you work towards a common goal.

Have a game night: A game night is a fun and low-key way to spend quality time together. Choose games that you both enjoy, whether that's a classic board game or a video game. The goal is to have fun and enjoy each other's company.

Cook a meal together: Cooking a meal together can be a great way to bond over a shared activity. Choose a recipe you're both interested in trying, and work together to prepare the meal. Then, remember to enjoy the fruits of your labor by sitting down to a nice dinner together.

Attend a concert or show: Attending a concert or show together can be a fun way to experience something new and create shared memories. Choose an artist or performance you both enjoy, and make a night of it.

Have a technology-free day: In today's world, it can be easy to get caught up in technology and social media. Taking a day to disconnect from technology can be a great way to focus on your relationship and connect with each other on a deeper level. Spend the day engaging in activities that don't involve technology, such as taking a hike or having a picnic.

Take a dance class: Learning to dance together can be a fun and romantic way to connect with your partner. Consider taking a salsa or ballroom dance class together, and enjoy getting close and moving together.

Create art together: Whether painting, drawing, or pottery, creating art together can be a great way to strengthen your bond and express your creativity. Choose an art form that you're both interested in, and enjoy the process of creating something together.

Go on a hike: Taking a hike together can be a great way to get outside and enjoy nature. Choose a trail you're both interested in, and spend the day exploring together.

Volunteer together: Volunteering can be a rewarding way to give back to your community and strengthen your bond as a couple. Consider volunteering at a local food bank or animal shelter, and enjoy the opportunity to work together towards a common goal.

Remember, the key to strengthening your bond as a couple is prioritizing your relationship and making time for each other. By engaging in activities that you both enjoy and focusing on building a deeper connection, you can create a strong and fulfilling partnership that will last a lifetime.

WEEK 7: MAINTAINING A SECURE AND EMOTIONALLY CONNECTED RELATIONSHIP

Being in a secure and emotionally connected relationship is an ideal that many people strive for. Everyone wants a relationship where both partners feel safe, supported, and validated in their emotions and experiences. This type of relationship requires open and honest communication, mutual respect, and a willingness to work through challenges together. In this essay, we will explore what it means to be in a secure and emotionally connected relationship and how couples can cultivate these qualities in their relationships.

A secure and emotionally connected relationship is one where both partners feel a sense of safety and security. This means that they are able to be vulnerable and share their innermost thoughts and feelings with each other without fear of judgment or rejection. Also, partners can rely on each other for emotional support and validation, which helps to build trust and a sense of closeness.

Open and honest communication is one of the key factors in creating a secure and emotionally connected relationship. This means that both partners feel comfortable expressing their thoughts and feelings, even when they feel uncomfortable. In a secure relationship, partners feel heard and understood by each other, and they can work through conflicts and challenges constructively and respectfully.

Another important factor is mutual respect. This means that both partners value each other's feelings, opinions, and needs and try to prioritize each other in their lives, which helps partners feel appreciated and valued, building a sense of security and trust.

In addition to open communication and mutual respect, a secure and emotionally connected relationship requires a willingness to work through challenges together. This means both partners are committed to the relationship and willing to overcome obstacles and build a stronger connection. In addition, in a secure relationship, partners feel supported and encouraged by each other, even in difficult times.

A strong emotional bond between partners is one of the hallmarks of a secure and emotionally connected relationship. This bond is built on a foundation of trust, respect, and open communication, and it allows partners to feel connected and supported by each other on a deep level.

Couples can cultivate a secure and emotionally connected relationship by focusing on several key factors. The first is communication; partners should communicate openly and honestly, even when it is difficult to do so. This means actively listening to each other, expressing empathy and understanding, and being willing to compromise solutions to conflicts.

Another important factor is trust. Couples should build trust in their relationship by being reliable, consistent, and transparent with each other. This means following through on commitments, being truthful and honest, and being accountable for one's actions.

In addition to communication and trust, couples can cultivate an emotionally connected relationship by practicing empathy and compassion towards each other. This means being aware of each other's feelings and needs and trying to understand and validate them. It also means offering support and comfort when one partner is going through a difficult time.

Finally, couples can cultivate a secure relationship by prioritizing each other in their lives. This means making time for each other, sharing experiences and interests, and trying to stay connected and engaged with each other. It also means being willing to make sacrifices and compromises for the sake of the relationship and being committed to working through challenges and conflicts together.

Being in a secure and emotionally connected relationship is an ideal that requires a commitment to open communication, mutual respect, and a willingness to work through challenges together. Couples can cultivate these qualities by focusing on communication, trust, and empathy.

Implementing Self-Care Practices

One of the most important ways to create and maintain a secure and emotionally connected relationship is to promote self-care and self-reflection practices.

Self-care is a set of activities and practices individuals undertake to maintain and improve their physical, mental, and emotional well-being. It involves taking deliberate actions to address one's own needs, prioritize one's health and happiness, and manage stress and other challenges that come with daily life.

Self-care activities can be simple or complex and vary depending on an individual's needs and preferences. Examples of self-care activities include exercising, eating well, getting enough sleep, taking time to relax and recharge, spending time with loved ones, practicing mindfulness or meditation, seeking therapy or counseling, setting boundaries and saying "no" when necessary, and engaging in hobbies and activities that bring joy and fulfillment.

Self-care is important because it helps individuals avoid burnout, reduce stress, improve their mood and overall health, and increase their resilience in facing challenges. When individuals prioritize self-care, they can better care for others, perform well in their work and personal lives, and live more fulfilling and enjoyable lives.

However, self-care is not always easy or straightforward. Many individuals may struggle to prioritize their own needs or feel guilty about taking time for themselves. Additionally, some individuals may not have access to the resources or support they need to engage in self-care activities. Therefore, it is important for individuals to identify their own needs and barriers to self-care and to seek help and support when necessary.

Self-care is not a one-time event or a quick fix but rather a continuous process of taking care of oneself. It requires commitment, consistency, and effort, but the benefits of self-care are well worth it. By prioritizing self-care, individuals can improve their health and well-being and live a more fulfilling and meaningful life.

Effects of Self-Care on a Relationship

Personal self-care can have a significant impact on romantic relationships. When individuals care for themselves, they can show their best selves in their relationships. This can lead to healthier communication, increased emotional intimacy, and a deeper connection with their partners.

Here are some ways in which personal self-care can affect romantic relationships:

Increased emotional resilience: When individuals engage in regular self-care activities such as exercise, mindfulness or meditation, and therapy, they can build emotional resilience. This means they are better equipped to handle their romantic relationships' stress, conflicts, and challenges. As a result, they are less likely to become overwhelmed or reactive and can better respond to their partners calmly and thoughtfully.

Improved communication: Engaging in self-care can also improve communication in romantic relationships. When individuals care for their emotional needs, they are less likely to project their insecurities or frustrations onto their partners. They can also communicate their needs and feelings more clearly and respectfully.

Enhanced emotional intimacy: Personal self-care can also enhance emotional intimacy in romantic relationships. When individuals can be vulnerable and share their emotions with their partners, it can create a deeper connection and sense of closeness. This can lead to greater trust, empathy, and understanding between partners.

Increased attraction: When individuals prioritize self-care and care for their physical and emotional well-being, they become more attractive to their partners. Feeling good about oneself can increase confidence, which can be very attractive to a romantic partner.

In contrast, when individuals neglect their personal self-care, it can negatively affect their romantic relationships. They may become irritable, distant, or withdrawn, which can strain the relationship. They may also have difficulty communicating their needs or responding to their partners healthily.

In conclusion, personal self-care can positively impact romantic relationships by increasing emotional resilience, improving communication, enhancing emotional intimacy, and increasing attraction. In addition, individuals can show their best selves in their relationships by prioritizing their needs, leading to a more fulfilling and satisfying romantic partnership.

How to Promote Self Care

Here are some ways to promote self-care:

Prioritize sleep: Getting enough sleep is essential for physical and mental health. Aim for 7-9 hours of sleep per night and establish a consistent bedtime routine.

Exercise regularly: Exercise is a great way to boost physical and mental health. Find a form of exercise you enjoy and make it a regular part of your routine.

Eat a healthy diet: Fuel your body with a balanced and nutritious diet. Eat plenty of fruits, vegetables, whole grains, and lean proteins.

Practice mindfulness or meditation: Mindfulness and meditation are practices that are often used interchangeably, but they are slightly different.

Mindfulness is being present and aware in the moment without judgment. It involves paying attention to your thoughts, feelings, and bodily sensations with curiosity and openness. Mindfulness can be practiced informally throughout the day by simply bringing awareness to your everyday experiences or through exercises such as mindful breathing, body scans, or mindful walking.

Meditation, on the other hand, is a more structured practice that involves setting aside time to focus the mind and cultivate specific qualities such as concentration, relaxation, or compassion. Meditation can take many forms, including seated meditation, movement meditation, or chanting. Meditation aims to train the mind to be more focused, calm, and aware.

Both mindfulness and meditation have been shown to have numerous benefits for physical and mental health, including reducing stress, anxiety, and depression, improving sleep quality and enhancing overall well-being. They can also improve cognitive function and increase emotional resilience.

Incorporating mindfulness and meditation into your daily routine can be as simple as taking a few minutes each day to breathe deeply and bring awareness to your present experience. There are many resources available, including books, apps, and guided meditations, that can help you develop a mindfulness or meditation practice.

Seek therapy or counseling: Therapy or counseling is a form of mental health treatment that involves talking with a trained professional to address personal or emotional issues. Therapy aims to help individuals better understand their thoughts, feelings, and behaviors and develop coping strategies to manage challenges and improve their quality of life.

Therapy can take many forms, including individual, couples, or family therapy, and can be delivered by licensed therapists, psychologists, or counselors. The type of therapy used will depend on the individual's specific needs and concerns.

Therapy can be helpful for a wide range of mental health concerns, including depression, anxiety, trauma, relationship issues, and addiction. It can also benefit individuals going through a difficult life transition, such as a divorce or the loss of a loved one.

It can provide a safe and supportive environment for individuals to explore their emotions and experiences without fear of judgment or criticism. It can also help individuals develop new skills and perspectives to navigate life's challenges and build more fulfilling relationships.

It's important to note that therapy is not a one-size-fits-all solution and may not be appropriate for everyone. However, if you're struggling with mental health concerns, therapy can be a valuable resource to help you develop the skills and strategies you need to live a healthy and fulfilling life. If you're interested in therapy, talk to your doctor or mental health professional about your options.

Establish boundaries: Setting boundaries with others can help you prioritize your needs and reduce stress.

Say "no" when necessary: Learning to say "no" is important to self-care and setting healthy boundaries. Saying "no" can help you prioritize your own needs and avoid overcommitting yourself, which can lead to stress and burnout.

Here are some tips to help you learn to say "no":

Be clear and direct: When saying "no," it's important to be clear and direct to avoid confusion. Use a firm but polite tone to communicate your decision.

Be honest: If you're saying "no" because you don't have the time or energy, it's okay to be honest. You don't need to provide a lengthy explanation; transparency can help others understand your decision.

Don't over-explain: While it's important, to be honest, you don't need to provide a detailed explanation for your decision. Instead, keep your response simple and to the point.

Offer an alternative: If you're saying "no" to a request, consider offering an alternative solution. For example, if someone asks you to help with a project but you don't have the time, you could connect them with someone who might be able to assist.

Practice saying "no": Learning to say "no" can take time and practice. Start with small requests and work your way up to more significant ones.

Remember your priorities: When deciding whether to say "yes" or "no," consider whether the request aligns with your priorities and values.

Don't feel guilty: It's natural to feel guilty when saying "no," but remember that prioritizing your needs is important for your well-being. You have the right to set boundaries and say "no" when necessary.

Learning to say "no" can be challenging, but it's important to self-care and setting healthy boundaries. With practice and patience, you can become more comfortable with this skill and better prioritize your needs.

Spend time in nature: Spending time outdoors can improve mental health and reduce stress.

Connect with loved ones: Cultivate meaningful relationships with friends and family members.

Practice self-compassion: Self-compassion is an essential aspect of self-care that involves treating yourself with kindness, understanding, and support. Here are some ways to practice self-compassion:

Be mindful of your self-talk: Pay attention to how you talk to yourself, and replace negative self-talk with positive and compassionate self-talk. Treat yourself like you would treat a friend going through a difficult time.

Practice self-care: Take care of yourself physically, emotionally, and mentally. Eat well, exercise, get enough sleep, and engage in activities that bring you joy and relaxation.

Accept your imperfections: Recognize that everyone makes mistakes and has flaws. Instead of criticizing yourself for your imperfections, practice self-acceptance and embrace your unique qualities.

Set realistic expectations: Avoid setting unrealistic goals or comparing yourself to others. Instead, set achievable goals and celebrate your accomplishments, no matter how small they may seem.

Practice gratitude: Focus on the positive things in your life and practice gratitude for the things you have. This can help shift your mindset from negative self-talk to a more positive and compassionate outlook.

Practice forgiveness: Forgive yourself for past mistakes and let go of self-blame. Instead, focus on learning from your experiences and moving forward with compassion and understanding.

Practicing self-compassion can be challenging at first, but it's an essential aspect of self-care that can lead to greater self-awareness, resilience, and well-being. Remember to treat yourself with kindness and understanding, and be patient as you continue your self-care journey.

Engage in hobbies or activities that bring joy: Make time for activities you enjoy and that bring you pleasure.

Take breaks when necessary: Take time off work or other obligations when you need a break or feel overwhelmed.

Engage in creative expression: Creative expression can be a powerful form of self-care that allows you to explore your emotions, reduce stress, and tap into your inner creativity. Here are some ways to incorporate creative expression into your self-care routine:

Journaling: Writing in a journal is a great way to explore your thoughts and emotions. You can write about anything on your mind, from daily events to deeper feelings and concerns.

Art-making: Whether painting, drawing, or sculpting, creating art can be a powerful way to express yourself and reduce stress. You don't need to be a professional artist to enjoy the benefits of art-making.

Music-making: Playing an instrument, singing, or composing music can be a great way to tap into your creative side and express yourself through sound.

Photography: Photography is another form of creative expression that can help you explore the world around you and capture meaningful moments.

Dance: Dancing is a fun and expressive way to move your body and connect with your emotions. You don't need to be a professional dancer to enjoy the benefits of moving to music.

Writing: Writing poetry, short stories, or even a novel can be a powerful way to explore your imagination and express your thoughts and feelings.

Crafting: Whether knitting, sewing, or making jewelry, crafting can be a relaxing and fulfilling way to express creativity.

Engaging in creative expression can help you connect with yourself on a deeper level and reduce stress and anxiety. It's important to remember that creative expression is a personal journey, and there's no right or wrong way to explore your creativity. Find an activity that resonates with you and make it a regular part of your self-care routine.

Self-reflection: Self-reflection is the process of looking inward and examining your thoughts, feelings, and behaviors. It involves stepping back from your day-to-day activities and examining your actions and motivations. Self-reflection can help you better understand yourself, your values, and your goals. It can also help you identify areas for growth.

Intentional Effort

Another technique that helps build and maintain secure and emotionally connected relationships is intentional effort.

An intentional effort is a deliberate and purposeful action toward achieving a specific goal or objective. It involves consciously putting in the necessary work and energy to reach a desired outcome. It also requires focus, motivation, and a clear understanding of what needs to be done to achieve the desired result.

For example, if someone wants to improve their physical fitness, they may need to make intentional efforts to exercise regularly, eat a healthy diet, and get enough rest. This would involve setting specific goals, creating a plan, and committing to the necessary actions to achieve those goals.

Intentional effort can also involve developing new habits and behaviors that support your goals. For example, if someone wants to improve their productivity, they may need to intentionally focus on developing habits such as time management, prioritization, and focus.

An intentional effort is important to personal growth and development. It requires self-discipline and a willingness to make sacrifices in the short term to achieve long-term goals. However, the benefits of intentional effort can be significant, including increased confidence, improved self-esteem, and a sense of accomplishment.

Intentional Effort in Relationships

Intentional effort is also important in relationships, as it involves consciously improving and strengthening the relationship. This requires deliberate and purposeful action toward understanding and meeting your partner's needs, communicating effectively, and building trust and intimacy.

Here are some important ways to show intentional effort in relationships:

Prioritize communication

Prioritizing communication in a relationship involves prioritizing communicating regularly with your partner in an open, honest, and respectful way. Here are some tips to help you prioritize communication in your relationship:

Schedule regular check-ins: Set aside time each day or week to check in with your partner and have meaningful conversations.

Avoid distractions: During conversations with your partner, minimize distractions, such as phones or television, to show that you are fully present and attentive.

Use "I" statements: When expressing your thoughts and feelings, use "I" statements to take responsibility for your feelings and avoid blaming or accusing your partner.

Be honest and transparent: Be honest and transparent with your partner about your thoughts, feelings, and needs.

Communicate your boundaries: Communicate your boundaries clearly and respect your partner's boundaries.

Use non-verbal communication: Use non-verbal cues such as eye contact, facial expressions, and body language to show interest and engagement in the conversation.

Be patient and understanding: Be patient and understanding with your partner, especially during difficult conversations, and avoid becoming defensive or critical.

By prioritizing communication in your relationship, you can strengthen your connection with your partner and improve the overall health of your relationship.

Practice forgiveness

Forgiveness in relationships is letting go of anger, resentment, or negative feelings towards your partner for something they have done or failed to do. It involves releasing the hurt or offense and moving forward positively.

As mentioned before, forgiveness does not mean forgetting the hurt or excusing the behavior that caused it. Instead, it is a personal decision that allows you to let go of negative emotions and heal from the pain caused by the offense.

Forgiveness can have many benefits in a relationship, including:

Rebuilding trust: Forgiveness can help rebuild trust in a relationship by showing your partner that you are willing to let go of the past and move forward.

Strengthening the relationship: By letting go of negative emotions, forgiveness can help strengthen the bond between partners and create a deeper connection.

Improving communication: Forgiveness can open communication channels between partners and allow for more honest and open conversations.

Reducing stress: Holding onto negative emotions can be stressful and draining, while forgiveness can bring peace and relief.

Promoting personal growth: Forgiveness can promote personal growth by allowing you to learn from past experiences and move forward positively.

Forgiveness is a personal choice and can take time and effort to achieve. It involves acknowledging the pain and hurt caused by the offense, allowing yourself to feel and process your emotions, and then making a conscious decision to let go of the negative feelings and move forward.

Spend quality time together

Quality time in relationships refers to the intentional and meaningful time spent together by partners. It is when partners give their undivided attention to each other and engage in activities they enjoy.

Some examples of activities that can be considered quality time include:

Going on a date: This can involve anything from going out to dinner or a movie to taking a walk or going to a museum.

Engaging in a shared hobby: Finding a shared hobby, such as cooking or hiking, can be a great way to spend quality time together.

Having a meaningful conversation: Carving out time to have a conversation about important topics can be a great way to deepen your connection.

Taking a vacation: Planning a trip together can be a way to create lasting memories and deepen your bond.

Quality time can vary depending on the couple's interests and preferences. The key is to make sure that the time spent together is intentional, meaningful, and focused on connecting with each other.

Be supportive

Being supportive in a relationship means being there for your partner through both the good and bad times. It means you are willing to offer help, encouragement, and emotional support when your partner needs it.

Here are some ways to be supportive in a relationship:

Listening actively: Being a good listener is important to be supportive. When your partner is going through a tough time, make sure to listen actively and empathetically without interrupting or judging.

Offering emotional support: Emotional support can come in many forms, such as offering a kind word, a hug, or a shoulder to cry on. It involves showing your partner that you care and is there for them.

Providing practical help: Sometimes, being supportive means helping your partner with practical tasks, such as cooking dinner or running errands, especially if they are going through a tough time or feeling overwhelmed.

Celebrating successes: Being supportive means celebrating your partner's successes and accomplishments, no matter how big or small. It involves showing pride in their achievements and offering encouragement for future endeavors.

Being non-judgmental: Being supportive entails being non-judgmental and accepting your partner for who they are. It involves creating a safe space for your partner to be themselves and to share their thoughts and feelings without fear of judgment.

Encouraging growth: Being supportive means encouraging your partner to grow and pursue their goals. It involves offering constructive feedback, setting achievable goals, and providing the necessary resources to help them achieve success.

Being supportive in a relationship requires empathy, compassion, and a willingness to put your partner's needs before your own at times. In addition, it can strengthen the bond between partners and create a deeper sense of intimacy and connection.

Share responsibilities

Sharing responsibilities in a relationship means dividing tasks and duties in a fair and equitable way for both partners. It involves recognizing that both partners have different strengths and weaknesses and finding ways to work together to achieve common goals.

Here are some tips for sharing responsibilities in a relationship:

Communicate openly: It's important to have open and honest communication about each partner's strengths, weaknesses, and preferences regarding household tasks and responsibilities. This can help avoid misunderstandings and build trust.

Create a list: Making a list of all the tasks that need to be done regularly, such as grocery shopping, cleaning, and paying bills, can help both partners to see what needs to be done and divide the tasks fairly.

Divide tasks fairly: Each partner should take on responsibilities that match their strengths and interests. This can help ensure that the workload is shared equally and that both partners feel valued.

Set boundaries: It's important to set clear boundaries around responsibilities so that both partners know what is expected of them. This can help avoid conflicts and misunderstandings.

Be flexible: Flexibility is key when it comes to sharing responsibilities in a relationship. Both partners should be willing to adjust their roles and responsibilities as needed based on changing circumstances.

Show appreciation: It's important to acknowledge and appreciate each other's efforts when sharing responsibilities. This can help build a sense of teamwork and create a more positive and supportive atmosphere in the relationship.

Sharing responsibilities in a relationship can help create a more balanced and equitable partnership leading to greater satisfaction and happiness for both partners. It's important to approach this topic with open communication, flexibility, and a willingness to work together to find solutions that work for everyone.

Learn their love language

Love language is a concept introduced by Dr. Gary Chapman in his book, "The 5 Love Languages: The Secret to Love That Lasts". It refers to the different ways in which people express and experience love. According to Chapman, there are five main love languages:

Words of affirmation: This love language involves using words to express love, appreciation, and affection. For example, saying "I love you," giving compliments, and expressing gratitude.

Acts of service: This love language involves doing things for your partner that you know they would appreciate. Examples include cooking a meal, doing the laundry, or running errands.

Receiving gifts: This love language involves giving and receiving gifts to express love and appreciation. It's not about the material value of the gift but rather the thought and effort behind it.

Quality time: This love language involves spending time with your partner, giving them your undivided attention, and engaging in meaningful conversations and activities together.

Physical touch: This love language involves expressing love and affection through physical touches, such as holding hands, hugging, and kissing.

Understanding your partner's love language and expressing love in a way that resonates with them can help strengthen your relationship and deepen your emotional connection. It's important to communicate openly and listen actively to your partner's needs and preferences when expressing love.

Activity: Maintaining a Secure and Emotionally Connected Relationship

Maintaining emotional intimacy is an important aspect of any healthy relationship. While it may seem challenging to find the time and energy to prioritize your relationship in today's busy world, it's important to make an effort to do so. There are many activities that couples can do to maintain emotional intimacy and strengthen their relationship. Here are some ideas:

Date Nights: Schedule regular date nights to spend quality time together. Date nights don't have to be elaborate or expensive; they can be as simple as cooking a meal together at home or going for a walk in the park. The important thing is to set aside time to focus on each other and enjoy each other's company.

Express Gratitude: Take time to express appreciation for each other regularly. This can be through small gestures like leaving a note, sending a text message, or more significant acts like planning a surprise for your partner. The key is to show your partner that you value and appreciate them.

Share Experiences: Try new things together, whether exploring a new hobby, traveling to a new place, or attending a cultural event. Sharing experiences can help you bond as a couple and create new memories together.

Communicate Openly: Make sure to communicate openly and honestly with your partner about your thoughts, feelings, and needs. This can help prevent misunderstandings and build trust. Set aside time to have regular conversations with your partner, and actively listen to what they say.

Engage in Physical Touch: Physical touch is important to maintain emotional intimacy. This can include holding hands, hugging, kissing, and cuddling. Even small acts of physical touch can help strengthen the emotional connection between partners.

Practice Active Listening: Listen actively when your partner speaks and show genuine interest in what they have to say. This can help them feel heard and understood, which is essential for building emotional intimacy.

Practice Empathy: Put yourself in your partner's shoes and try to see things from their perspective. This can help you understand their needs and feelings better and respond in a more supportive way.

Plan Special Occasions: Celebrate special occasions like birthdays, anniversaries, and holidays together. Planning special occasions together can be a fun way to create new memories and strengthen your emotional connection.

Take Time Apart: While spending time together is important, it's also important to take time apart to pursue individual interests and hobbies. This can help you maintain your identity while keeping your relationship strong.

Practice Forgiveness: Forgiveness is an essential part of any healthy relationship. When conflicts arise, make an effort to forgive your partner and move forward together.

Support Each Other's Goals: Show support for each other's goals and dreams, even if they differ from yours. This can help you both feel valued and supported in the relationship.

Create Rituals: Create rituals or traditions that you can do together regularly. This can be as simple as having coffee every morning or walking together after dinner.

Prioritize Intimacy: Make sure to prioritize intimacy in your relationship, whether physical or emotional. Schedule time for intimacy and make an effort to connect with your partner on a regular basis.

Seek Professional Help: If you're struggling with maintaining emotional intimacy in your relationship, seek the help of a professional. A therapist or counselor can help you resolve any issues and strengthen your emotional connection.

Practice Mindfulness: Practice mindfulness together, whether it's through meditation, yoga, or another practice. This can help you both stay present and connected in the relationship.

In conclusion, maintaining emotional intimacy is essential for any healthy relationship. Taking the time to engage in activities that show your good intentions to your partner can help strengthen your relationship and make it worthwhile and meaningful.

WEEK 8: INTIMACY AND ROMANCE

Intimacy and romance are two aspects of human relationships that are often intertwined but can also be experienced independently. While intimacy refers to the emotional and physical closeness between two individuals, romance involves the feelings of love and attraction associated with a romantic relationship. Both intimacy and romance play important roles in our lives, influencing our emotional well-being and quality of life. In this chapter, we will explore the concepts of intimacy and romance in greater detail, examining their psychological, social, and cultural dimensions.

Intimacy can be described as the ability to share one's deepest thoughts, feelings, and experiences with another person. It involves a sense of emotional vulnerability and the willingness to open up and be honest with someone else. Also, it can be experienced in many different types of relationships, including friendships, familial relationships, and romantic partnerships. In romantic relationships, intimacy is often associated with physical closeness, such as hugging, kissing, and sexual activity. However, emotional intimacy is equally important and involves sharing one's innermost thoughts and feelings with a partner without fear of judgment or rejection.

One of the most significant benefits of intimacy is that it can promote feelings of happiness, contentment, and fulfillment in our lives. When we feel connected to others on a deep emotional level, we experience a sense of belonging and purpose that can enhance our overall well-being. Intimacy can also help us feel more confident and secure in ourselves, allowing us to share our strengths and weaknesses with another person who accepts and supports us.

However, intimacy can also be challenging to achieve, particularly in our fast-paced and often disconnected modern world. In many cases, individuals may struggle to connect with others on a deep level due to past traumas, fears of vulnerability, or simply a lack of social skills. Some people may also struggle with intimacy in romantic relationships due to past experiences of heartbreak or betrayal. In these cases, it can be helpful to seek the assistance of a mental health professional or relationship counselor who can provide guidance and support in developing healthy intimacy skills.

Romance, on the other hand, is a distinct aspect of human relationships that involves feelings of love, attraction, and desire. While intimacy can exist in platonic relationships, romance is typically reserved for romantic partnerships. Romance involves a variety of emotions, including infatuation, passion, and affection. Moreover, it can be experienced in different ways, for example, through physical touch, verbal expressions of love, and acts of kindness and affection.

Like intimacy, romance is essential in our lives, contributing to our overall happiness. Romantic relationships can provide us with a sense of companionship, support, and love that can enhance our lives in many ways. In addition, research has shown that people who are in happy, committed relationships tend to experience better mental and physical health outcomes than those who are single or in unhappy relationships.

And just like intimacy, it can also be hard to achieve, particularly in a world where social norms and expectations can sometimes pressure individuals to conform to certain relationship ideals. For example, there may be pressure to find a partner who meets specific physical or social criteria or follow traditional gender roles in the relationship. These expectations can create stress and anxiety for individuals who do not meet these standards and may lead to feelings of loneliness and isolation.

One of the most significant challenges of romance is navigating the complexities of human attraction and desire. While physical attraction is often a key component of romantic relationships, it can also be a source of confusion and frustration. Many people struggle with feelings of attraction to individuals who may not be a good match for them in other ways, such as personality or values. Others may struggle with balancing their desire for physical intimacy with their need for emotional connection and trust.

Lack of intimacy and romance in a relationship can lead to a variety of issues, both emotional and physical. Here are some of the common issues that may arise:

Emotional distance: Emotional distance can occur when there is a lack of intimacy and romance in a relationship. This means that partners may feel disconnected or detached from each other, leading to feelings of loneliness, isolation, and dissatisfaction.

Decreased satisfaction: Without intimacy and romance, partners may feel less satisfied with their relationship. They start to feel unfulfilled, unappreciated or neglected, which leads to resentment and frustration.

Decreased attraction: Intimacy and romance are important factors in attraction between partners. When these aspects are lacking, partners may feel less attracted to each other, leading to a decreased desire for physical intimacy and potentially leading to infidelity.

Stress and anxiety: The absence of intimacy and romance in a relationship can create stress and anxiety for partners. They may worry about the state of their relationship, feel insecure about their partner's feelings, or feel overwhelmed by the effort required to improve the relationship.

Physical health issues: Lack of intimacy and romance can also lead to physical health issues. For example, individuals may experience increased stress levels, which can lead to high blood pressure, heart disease, and other health problems.

Mental health issues: A lack of intimacy and romance can also lead to mental health issues, such as depression and anxiety. Partners may feel hopeless or desperate about their relationship, leading to sadness and distress.

Infertility: In some cases, a lack of intimacy and romance can lead to infertility. It can occur when partners are not having regular sexual intercourse, which leads to decreased fertility over time.

Overall, a lack of intimacy and romance can lead to various negative consequences for partners. Therefore, it is important to address these issues early on in the relationship and work to improve intimacy and romance to prevent these negative outcomes. To do that, you need to learn the concepts of intimacy and apply different techniques to maintain a healthy intimacy level.

TYPES OF INTIMACY IN A HEALTHY RELATIONSHIP

EMOTIONAL INTIMACY

Emotional intimacy in a relationship refers to the closeness, trust, and vulnerability that two individuals share with each other. It is the ability to be open and honest with your partner about your deepest thoughts, feelings, fears, and desires and to feel accepted and understood by them.

Emotional intimacy involves sharing your innermost self with your partner, knowing that they will listen to you without judgment, and responding with empathy and compassion. It involves feeling safe enough to share your vulnerabilities and being able to support your partner in the same way.

When partners have emotional intimacy, they feel connected deeply, creating a sense of closeness and security in the relationship. Therefore, emotional intimacy is essential for a healthy relationship, as it allows partners to develop trust, build a strong bond, and feel fulfilled.

INTELLECTUAL INTIMACY

Intellectual intimacy in a relationship refers to the ability of two individuals to share their thoughts, ideas, and perspectives in a profound and meaningful way. It involves engaging in conversations that challenge and stimulate each other's minds and exploring new ideas and concepts together.

Intellectual intimacy is not just about having similar interests or being knowledgeable about the same topics but rather about understanding and respecting each other's intellectual abilities and perspectives. It involves expressing oneself freely without fear of being judged and being open to learning from one's partner.

When partners have intellectual intimacy, they can engage in stimulating conversations and debates that lead to personal growth and mutual understanding. They can learn from each other's experiences and perspectives and share mutual respect for each other's intellect. This type of intimacy can enhance the emotional connection between partners as they learn to appreciate and value each other's unique perspectives and insights.

Physical intimacy

Physical intimacy in a relationship refers to the physical closeness and connection between partners. It can involve a range of physical acts, including holding hands, hugging, kissing, cuddling, and sexual activity.

Physical intimacy is an important aspect of a healthy romantic relationship, as it allows partners to express their love and affection for each other tangibly. In addition, it can create a sense of intimacy and closeness between partners and help build and maintain emotional connections.

Physical intimacy can also provide many health benefits, both physical and emotional. For example, it can release feel-good hormones like oxytocin, reduce stress levels, and boost immune function. It can also enhance emotional well-being and promote feelings of happiness and satisfaction.

However, it's important to note that physical intimacy should always be consensual and respectful. It's essential to communicate openly with your partner about your boundaries and preferences and to always prioritize each other's comfort and safety.

Gottman's approach to maintaining romance

The Gottman Method is a couples therapy approach developed by Drs. John and Julie Gottman. It is a research-based approach that focuses on improving communication, understanding, and the overall quality of the relationship. The method is designed to help couples strengthen their relationship by addressing issues related to emotional intimacy, conflict resolution, and relationship building.

The Gottman Method is based on over four decades of research and has been extensively tested and refined. The approach focuses on seven essential principles for a healthy and successful relationship.

These principles include building love maps, nurturing fondness and admiration, turning toward each other instead of away, having a positive perspective, managing conflict, making life dreams come true, and creating shared meaning.

The first principle of the Gottman Method is building love maps. It involves knowing each other's world, including likes, dislikes, and life goals. Couples can build a stronger bond by creating a strong foundation of understanding and knowing each other.

The second principle is nurturing fondness and admiration. It involves expressing appreciation and affection toward each other, focusing on the positive aspects of the relationship, and building a sense of fondness and affection.

The third principle is turning toward each other instead of away, which means being responsive to each other's needs, supporting each other emotionally, and being there for one's partner in times of need.

The fourth principle is the positive perspective. This principle involves seeing the best in each other and the relationship, even during times of conflict or stress.

The fifth principle is managing conflict. This principle entails learning to communicate effectively, listening to each other's concerns, and finding ways to resolve conflict in a healthy and constructive manner.

The sixth principle is making life dreams come true. It involves supporting each other's goals and aspirations and working together to achieve them.

The seventh principle is creating shared meaning. This principle involves building a sense of purpose and meaning in the relationship by creating traditions and rituals that strengthen the bond between partners.

The Gottman Method uses a range of techniques and exercises to help couples strengthen their relationship. These include learning effective communication skills, identifying and changing negative relationship patterns, and building intimacy and connection.

One of the key features of the Gottman Method is the use of assessments to help couples identify areas of strength and areas for improvement. These assessments include the Relationship Checkup, which helps couples identify the areas of their relationship that need attention, and the Love Maps Card Deck, which helps couples deepen their understanding of each other.

In summary, the Gottman Method is a comprehensive approach to couples therapy that emphasizes building a strong foundation of understanding, communication, and connection. It is grounded in extensive research and has been shown to be effective in helping couples improve their relationship satisfaction and overall well-being.

To delve deeper into the techniques that Gottman could recommend, here are a few activities to remember to keep intimacy and romance alive.

THE IMPORTANCE OF RITUALS AND ROUTINES

Rituals and routines play an essential role in maintaining healthy and happy relationships. They provide a sense of stability, comfort, and predictability that can help couples navigate the ups and downs of life together. Here are some reasons why rituals and routines are important in relationships:

Creating a sense of connection: Rituals and routines can create a deeper connection and intimacy between partners. Whether it's having a weekly date night or a morning coffee together, these activities can help couples bond and feel more connected.

Providing a sense of security: In a world that is often unpredictable and chaotic, rituals and routines can provide a sense of security and stability for couples. Knowing they have a set time to connect and spend together can be comforting and reassuring.

Promoting positive communication: Rituals and routines provide an opportunity for positive communication between partners. Whether it's discussing their day over dinner or sharing their thoughts and feelings during a morning walk, these activities can help couples communicate in a healthy and constructive way.

Building a shared history: Rituals and routines can create a sense of shared history and memories between partners. Whether it's a yearly vacation or a holiday tradition, these activities can create a sense of continuity and shared experiences that can strengthen the relationship.

Fostering personal growth: Rituals and routines can also provide personal growth and development opportunities. Whether it's working out or taking a class together, these activities can help couples grow and learn together, leading to a deeper sense of connection and intimacy.

Overall, rituals and routines can be an essential part of maintaining a healthy and happy relationship. They provide a sense of connection, security, and intimacy between partners and can help couples navigate the ups and downs of life together. Here are some examples of activities you can do together.

Regular date nights

Regular date nights are important for couples for several reasons:

Rekindling Romance: Date nights allow couples to rekindle the romance and intimacy in their relationship. They are times to focus on each other and to remind each other why you fell in love in the first place.

Quality Time: In today's fast-paced world, couples often find themselves juggling work, family, and other responsibilities, leaving little time for each other. Date nights allow couples to spend quality time together without distractions, providing an opportunity to deepen their connection.

Communication: Date nights are an excellent opportunity for couples to communicate and connect. They allow them to share their thoughts, feelings, and experiences in a relaxed and comfortable setting, helping to strengthen their emotional bond.

Variety and Fun: Regular date nights give couples a chance to try new things and have fun together. It could be trying a new restaurant, taking a cooking class, or attending a concert. Whatever activity you choose would help keep the relationship fresh and exciting.

Stress Relief: Date nights provide a break from the stresses of everyday life. They allow couples to step away from their daily responsibilities and focus on themselves, which can help reduce stress and improve mental health.

Commitment: Scheduling regular date nights shows a commitment to the relationship. It shows that both partners are willing to make time for each other and prioritize their relationship, which can help strengthen their bond.

Regular date nights are important for maintaining a healthy and happy relationship. It provides an opportunity for couples to rekindle romance, communicate, have fun, relieve stress, and show their commitment to each other. Couples can deepen their connection and strengthen their relationship by setting aside time for regular date nights.

Expressing appreciation and gratitude daily

Expressing appreciation and gratitude daily in a relationship is a powerful way to strengthen the bond between partners and cultivate a more positive and loving atmosphere. Here are some benefits of expressing appreciation and gratitude in a relationship:

Promotes positivity: Expressing appreciation and gratitude regularly promotes a more positive and loving atmosphere in the relationship. It helps to shift the focus away from negative aspects and towards the positive aspects of the relationship.

Increases intimacy: Regularly expressing appreciation and gratitude helps to build intimacy between partners. It creates a safe and comfortable environment where both partners feel valued and appreciated, which helps to deepen their emotional connection.

Boosts self-esteem: When partners express appreciation and gratitude for each other, it can boost their self-esteem and self-worth. It creates a sense of validation and appreciation, which can motivate continued positive behaviors and actions.

Reduces stress: Expressing appreciation and gratitude can help reduce relationship stress. It helps to create a more relaxed and positive environment, which helps alleviate stress and tension.

Strengthens the relationship: Regularly expressing appreciation and gratitude can help strengthen the relationship over time. It creates a positive feedback loop where partners feel appreciated and valued, which in turn, motivates them to continue positive behaviors and actions towards each other.

Some simple ways to express appreciation and gratitude daily in a relationship include:

- Saying "thank you" for the little things your partner does for you
- Giving your partner a compliment
- Writing a note of appreciation or gratitude
- Verbally expressing your appreciation and gratitude for your partner's qualities, actions, and efforts
- Doing something special or thoughtful for your partner

Expressing appreciation and gratitude daily in a relationship is a simple yet powerful way to strengthen the bond between partners, promote positivity, increase intimacy, boost self-esteem, reduce stress, and strengthen the overall relationship.

The Role of Small Gestures and Acts of Service

In a relationship, small gestures and acts of service can play a vital role in maintaining a strong, healthy, and fulfilling bond between partners. These actions help demonstrate love, appreciation, and care for one another on a daily basis.

Some examples of small gestures in a relationship include leaving a love note for your partner, making their favorite breakfast in bed, bringing them a cup of tea or coffee in the morning, or simply giving them a warm hug or kiss.

Acts of service can also be a powerful way to show love and support in a relationship. They include doing the dishes or laundry, running errands, cooking dinner, or helping with a project or task your partner is struggling with.

These small gestures and acts of service strengthen the emotional connection between partners, promote a sense of teamwork and collaboration, and create a positive, supportive environment for both individuals in the relationship.

The concept of the "6-second kiss" for daily connection

The "6-second kiss" is a simple but powerful concept that can help couples maintain a strong emotional connection. The idea is to take six seconds to give your partner a deep, meaningful kiss each day without any distractions or interruptions.

Research has shown that physical touch, like kissing, can release feel-good hormones like oxytocin and dopamine, which help reduce stress, boost mood, and improve overall well-being. By taking just six seconds to connect with your partner, you can help reinforce the emotional bond between you and your partner and create a sense of intimacy and closeness.

The "6-second kiss" is also a way to prioritize your relationship amid busy, stressful schedules. Connecting with your partner in this way can show them they are a priority in your life and help strengthen your commitment to one another.

EFT's perspective on emotional and physical intimacy

Emotion-focused therapy (EFT) is an approach to psychotherapy based on the idea that emotions are a primary source of information about ourselves and our experiences. As a result, they play a central role in our relationships and mental health. EFT was developed in the 1980s by Dr. Leslie Greenberg and Dr. Sue Johnson and has since been used to treat a wide range of emotional and relational issues.

EFT aims to help individuals and couples better understand and manage their emotions and use them as a guide for healing and growth. This method is practiced through a collaborative and empathic therapeutic relationship, where the therapist helps the client identify and express their emotions and explore the underlying thoughts, beliefs, and behaviors that may contribute to their emotional struggles.

Here are some concepts that EFT recommends to help build a more stable relationship:

Understanding attachment needs and fears

Attachment needs and fears are related to how we form and maintain close relationships with others, and they can play a significant role in our emotional well-being.

Attachment needs refer to the basic human desire to feel loved, secure, and connected to others. These needs are rooted in early childhood experiences and are shaped by our interactions with primary caregivers. They include feeling valued and respected, having a sense of trust and safety, and feeling emotionally connected to others.

Attachment fears, on the other hand, are the negative emotions and behaviors that arise when these needs are not met. Some common attachment fears include fear of abandonment, rejection, or loss of control. These fears can lead to various negative behaviors, such as clinginess, jealousy, or emotional withdrawal.

Understanding our own attachment needs and fears can be a valuable tool for promoting healthy relationships and emotional well-being. By identifying our attachment needs, we can take steps to ensure they are met in our relationships, such as communicating openly and honestly with our partners and setting healthy boundaries. Likewise, by recognizing our attachment fears, we can overcome them by challenging negative self-talk or seeking therapy to address deeper emotional wounds.

Ultimately, cultivating a deeper understanding of our attachment needs and fears can build stronger, more fulfilling relationships and lead emotionally satisfying lives.

Creating a secure base for exploring vulnerability and intimacy

Creating a secure base for exploring vulnerability and intimacy is essential for building strong, healthy relationships. A secure base is a foundation of trust, safety, and support that allows individuals to feel comfortable being vulnerable and opening up emotionally to their partners.

To create a secure base, it is important to first establish clear and healthy communication with your partner, which involves being open and honest about your needs and desires, as well as actively listening to and validating your partner's feelings and concerns.

It is also important to establish boundaries and guidelines for how you will interact with each other, such as setting aside dedicated time to connect and being mindful of each other's emotional needs.

Another key component of creating a secure base is building a foundation of mutual respect and trust. This means being consistent in your actions and words and showing that you can be relied upon to provide emotional support and comfort.

Finally, it is important to remember that creating a secure base for exploring vulnerability and intimacy is an ongoing process that requires continual effort and attention. It may involve taking risks and stepping outside of your comfort zone, but the rewards of a strong and fulfilling relationship can be well worth the effort.

Identifying and Addressing Blocks to Intimacy

Intimacy is an essential part of any healthy relationship, but sometimes, blocks or barriers may prevent individuals from experiencing true intimacy with their partner. These blocks can take many forms, including physical, emotional, mental, or spiritual barriers. Here are some common blocks to intimacy and ways to address them:

Fear of vulnerability: Being vulnerable and sharing our deepest thoughts and feelings with someone else can be scary, especially if we've been hurt in the past. To overcome this block, it's important to communicate openly and honestly with your partner about your fears and to work together to build a safe and trusting environment.

Negative self-talk: Negative self-talk and self-doubt can prevent individuals from feeling confident and comfortable in their own skin, which can impact their ability to connect intimately with their partner. Addressing negative self-talk may involve identifying and challenging negative beliefs, practicing self-compassion, and building self-confidence.

Lack of communication: A lack of communication can prevent individuals from building a deeper connection with their partner. It's important to set aside time to talk openly and honestly with your partner and actively listen and respond to their needs and concerns.

Trauma: Past trauma can create emotional blocks that prevent individuals from fully connecting with their partners. In these cases, seeking therapy or other professional support may be helpful to work through past trauma and heal from emotional wounds.

Busy schedules and distractions: Busy schedules and distractions can prevent individuals from making time for intimacy with their partner. It's important to prioritize intimacy and make time for it in your schedule, even if it means cutting back on other activities.

Sexual difficulties: Sexual difficulties, such as performance anxiety or lack of desire, can create barriers to intimacy. It's important to communicate openly with your partner about any sexual difficulties and to seek out professional support if needed.

Individuals and couples can create a more intimate and fulfilling relationship by identifying and addressing blocks to intimacy. It's important to approach these barriers with compassion and a willingness to work together to create a safe and loving environment for emotional connection.

Exercises and Activities to Reignite the Spark

Seeing that intimacy and romance are important pillars to building a sound relationship home, here are some of the most effective ways to rebuild and maintain the spark in your relationship.

"Love Languages" Exercise

Take a few moments to reflect on how you feel most loved and appreciated by others. Consider past experiences where you have felt particularly loved or cared for by someone else.

Review the five love languages: words of affirmation, quality time, receiving gifts, acts of service, and physical touch. Then, familiarize yourself with the descriptions and examples of each.

For each love language, ask yourself the following questions:

- How often do I feel loved when I receive this type of love language from others?
- How often do I express this type of love language to others?
- How important is this love language to me?

Based on your answers, rank each love language in order of importance to you, from most important to least important.

Reflect on what you have learned about your love language preferences. Consider how you can use this knowledge to better communicate your needs to others and to show love and appreciation to those around you.

And remember, everyone has a different love language preference, so it's important to communicate and understand each other's preferences to build stronger and more fulfilling relationships.

Intimacy-building questions: a list of conversation starters to deepen emotional connection

Here are some intimacy-building questions that you can use to deepen your connection with your partner:

- What was your favorite childhood memory?
- What is something that you've always wanted to try but have yet to have the opportunity to do?
- What is the most meaningful gift you have ever received, and why was it so important to you?
- What is your biggest fear, and how have you worked to overcome it?
- What is one thing that you appreciate about our relationship, and why?
- What is one thing you feel we could work on to strengthen our relationship?
- What is one thing you've learned from a past relationship that has helped you with our relationship?
- How do you like to express and receive love and affection?
- What are your goals and aspirations for the future, and how can we support each other in achieving them?
- What is one thing you have never shared with anyone else, and why?

The "Appreciation Jar"

The Appreciation Jar activity is a simple and fun way to express gratitude and appreciation for your partner, family member, or friend. Here's how to do it:

Find a jar or container and decorate it as you like. You can use stickers, paint, markers, or any other materials that you have on hand.

Cut small pieces of paper into strips and place them in a visible location along with a pen or marker.

Each day, take a few moments to write down something you appreciate about your partner or loved one and place it in the jar. This can be anything from a small gesture they did for you to a quality you admire about them or a moment you shared together.

Encourage your partner or loved one to do the same. You can either share the same jar or have separate jars for each person.

After a few weeks or months, set aside some time to read the notes together. This can be a great opportunity to reflect on your relationship and express gratitude for its positive aspects.

The Appreciation Jar activity is a simple but powerful way to cultivate gratitude and appreciation in your relationship. By taking the time to notice and acknowledge the positive aspects of your partner or loved one, you can deepen your emotional connection and build a stronger and more fulfilling relationship.

Sensate focus exercises

Sensate focus exercises are guided activities that can be used to enhance physical intimacy and connection between partners. They involve a series of steps that focus on developing greater awareness and sensitivity to touch and physical sensation. Here is a simple Sensate Focus exercise that you can try with your partner:

First, find a comfortable, private space where you won't be disturbed.

Begin by taking turns touching each other's hands, arms, and faces in a slow and deliberate manner. Focus on the sensation of touch and the feelings that arise as you touch and are touched.

After a few minutes of exploring each other's arms and faces, move on to the torso and legs. Continue to touch each other slowly and gently, paying attention to the sensations that arise.

As you touch each other, focus on your breath and the physical sensations in your body. Allow yourself to be fully present in the moment without any distractions or judgments.

After several minutes of touching each other's torso and legs, move on to more intimate areas of the body. Then, again, take turns exploring each other's bodies, paying attention to the sensations that arise.

Throughout the exercise, take breaks as needed to check in with each other and share your thoughts and feelings. Focus on the connection and intimacy that you are building with each other.

Sensate focus exercises can be a powerful tool for enhancing physical intimacy and connection between partners. By focusing on the present moment and developing greater awareness of physical sensation, you can deepen your emotional and physical connection with your partner.

USEFUL RESOURCES FOR ENHANCING INTIMACY AND ROMANCE

BOOKS:

"The Seven Principles for Making Marriage Work" by John Gottman

"The Seven Principles for Making Marriage Work" is a book by renowned psychologist John Gottman, based on his extensive research on marital relationships. The book provides practical advice and strategies for couples to build and maintain strong, healthy marriages. Here is a summary of the seven principles outlined in the book:

Enhance Your Love Maps: This principle focuses on the importance of knowing your partner's inner world, including their hopes, dreams, and fears. Building a detailed "love map" of your partner's inner life can deepen your understanding and connection with them.

Nurture Fondness and Admiration: This principle emphasizes the importance of cultivating positive feelings and emotions towards your partner. By focusing on their positive qualities and expressing admiration and appreciation, you can strengthen your emotional bond and protect your relationship from negativity.

Turn Towards Each Other Instead of Away: This principle emphasizes the importance of responding positively to your partner's bids for emotional connection rather than ignoring or rejecting them. By turning towards each other and responding with warmth and affection, you can build a strong foundation of trust and intimacy.

Let Your Partner Influence You: This principle emphasizes the importance of mutual respect and compromise in a relationship. You can build a stronger and more collaborative partnership by valuing your partner's opinions and being open to their influence.

Solve Your Solvable Problems: This principle focuses on developing effective problem-solving skills and communication techniques. By listening actively, expressing your needs clearly, and finding common ground, you can resolve conflicts and build a more harmonious relationship.

Overcome Gridlock: This principle addresses long-standing conflicts that seem impossible to resolve. By understanding the underlying emotional needs and beliefs that drive these conflicts and finding creative solutions that honor both partners' needs, you can break through gridlock and find new ways to connect.

Create Shared Meaning: This principle emphasizes creating a shared sense of purpose and meaning in your relationship. You can deepen your emotional connection and build a more fulfilling partnership by identifying shared values, traditions, and goals.

Overall, "The Seven Principles for Making Marriage Work" provides a comprehensive framework for building and maintaining a strong, healthy, and fulfilling marital relationship.

"Hold Me Tight: Seven Conversations for a Lifetime of Love" by Sue Johnson

"Hold Me Tight: Seven Conversations for a Lifetime of Love" by Sue Johnson is a book that focuses on the importance of emotional connection and attachment in intimate relationships. The book is based on Emotionally Focused Therapy (EFT) and offers readers a guide to understanding and improving their emotional bonds with their partner.

The book is divided into seven conversations, each focused on a different aspect of emotional connection, such as recognizing and understanding negative patterns, finding new ways to communicate and connect, and building a secure emotional bond with your partner. Throughout the book, Johnson uses real-life case examples and exercises to help readers apply the principles of EFT to their own relationships.

One of the book's key messages is that emotional connection is vital to a healthy and satisfying relationship. In addition, Johnson emphasizes the importance of identifying and addressing negative patterns of interaction, which can often develop due to attachment wounds or trauma from past relationships.

The book also provides practical advice on improving communication and building a stronger emotional bond with your partner. Johnson emphasizes the importance of expressing emotions openly and honestly and actively listening and responding to your partner's needs and concerns.

Overall, "Hold Me Tight" is a valuable resource for anyone looking to improve their emotional connection and attachment with their partner. In addition, the book offers a practical and accessible guide to EFT, which has been shown to be an effective approach to couples therapy.

"The 5 Love Languages: The Secret to Love that Lasts" by Gary Chapman

"The 5 Love Languages: The Secret to Love that Lasts" by Gary Chapman is a book that explores the concept of love languages and how understanding them can lead to stronger, more fulfilling relationships.

According to Chapman, people express and receive love differently, which he refers to as "love languages." These love languages are: words of affirmation, acts of service, receiving gifts, quality time, and physical touch. Understanding your own love language, as well as your partner's, can help you communicate your love and build a stronger emotional connection.

The book is divided into five sections, each focusing on one of the love languages. Chapman provides examples of how each love language might be expressed and practical tips for incorporating them into your relationship. He also discusses how to identify your love language and how to communicate it to your partner.

One of the key messages of the book is that expressing love in your partner's preferred love language can be more meaningful than expressing it in your own. For example, if your partner's love language is acts of service, doing something kind for them, like cooking dinner or cleaning the house, may be more meaningful than saying, "I love you."

Chapman emphasizes the importance of actively showing your partner love rather than assuming they already know how you feel. He also emphasizes that each partner may have a different love language and that understanding and respecting these differences is essential for building a strong and lasting relationship.

Podcasts:

"The Gottman Relationship Coach" by John and Julie Gottman

"The Gottman Relationship Coach" is a podcast hosted by renowned psychologists and relationship experts John and Julie Gottman. The podcast offers practical advice, tools, and strategies for couples to build and maintain healthy, satisfying relationships. Here is a summary of some of the key topics and themes covered in the podcast:

Building a Strong Foundation: Many episodes focus on building a strong foundation of trust, respect, and emotional connection in a relationship. The Gottmans offer practical tips for developing effective communication skills, expressing appreciation and gratitude, and nurturing positive emotions toward your partner.

Managing Conflict: Another major theme of the podcast is managing conflict and resolving disagreements healthily and constructively. The Gottmans offer insights into the emotional dynamics that underlie conflict and provide practical tools and strategies for de-escalating tension, listening actively, and finding common ground.

Enhancing Intimacy and Passion: The podcast also offers guidance on enhancing intimacy, connection, and passion in a long-term relationship. The Gottmans discuss the importance of physical affection, emotional attunement, and shared experiences in maintaining a satisfying and fulfilling relationship.

Strengthening Friendship and Fun: The Gottmans also emphasize the importance of maintaining a strong friendship and sense of fun in a relationship. They offer practical tips for cultivating shared interests and activities, maintaining a sense of playfulness and humor, and keeping the relationship fresh and exciting.

"Relationship Alive!" by Neil Sattin

"Relationship Alive!" is a podcast hosted by Neil Sattin that provides practical and insightful advice for building strong and healthy relationships. The podcast features a variety of guests, including relationship experts, therapists, and authors, who offer their expertise on topics such as communication, intimacy, and emotional connection.

Each episode of the podcast is structured around a particular theme, with Sattin often interviewing a guest expert on the topic. The conversations are conversational and in-depth, with the guests sharing their insights and offering practical advice for improving relationships.

Some common themes explored in the podcast include the importance of communication in relationships, understanding attachment styles and how they impact relationships, and how to cultivate emotional intimacy and connection.

Sattin also often includes listener questions and feedback in the podcast, making it more like a conversation between a community of people looking to improve their relationships.

One of the key messages of the podcast is that building strong and healthy relationships requires ongoing effort and communication. Sattin and his guests emphasize the importance of being open and honest with your partner, actively working to build trust and emotional connection, and being willing to learn and grow together as a couple.

APPS:

Gottman Card Decks

The Gottman Card Decks are a set of mobile apps designed to help couples build intimacy and connection in their relationships, created by relationship experts Drs. John and Julie Gottman, the Card Decks consist of several themed decks, each containing a series of open-ended questions and prompts for couples to explore together.

Currently, six different card decks are available, each with a specific focus. These include "Love Maps," "Open-Ended Questions," "Opinions and Preferences," "Debriefing and Stress-Reducing Conversation," "Expressing Needs," and "Salsa (Sex And Love Task Assessment)."

The Love Maps deck helps couples get to know each other on a deeper level by asking questions about each other's likes, dislikes, and life experiences. The Open-Ended Questions deck is designed to encourage conversation and explore each other's thoughts and feelings. The Opinions and Preferences deck focuses on exploring differences and similarities in tastes, values, and beliefs.

The Debriefing and Stress-Reducing Conversation deck prompts couples to process stressful or difficult experiences and emotions together. The Expressing Needs deck helps couples constructively communicate their needs and desires. Finally, the Salsa deck is designed to assess couples' sexual compatibility and explore ways to enhance intimacy and pleasure in the relationship.

Each deck includes a variety of cards with different prompts, allowing couples to choose the topics that are most relevant and interesting to them. In addition, the cards are designed to be used in a conversational and playful way, making it easier for couples to explore and connect with each other.

Overall, the Gottman Card Decks are a fun and engaging way for couples to deepen their emotional connection and build intimacy. The decks can be used independently or in conjunction with other Gottman resources, such as books, workshops, or therapy sessions.

Lasting

Lasting is a mobile app designed to help couples improve their relationships and build healthier partnerships. The app is based on cognitive-behavioral therapy (CBT) and mindfulness principles and was developed by a team of relationship experts and therapists.

Upon downloading the app, users are prompted to complete an assessment that evaluates various aspects of their relationship, such as communication, conflict resolution, intimacy, and trust. Based on the assessment results, the app creates a personalized relationship improvement plan that includes daily exercises, quizzes, and tips for improving the specific areas of the relationship that need attention.

The app includes a variety of features designed to help couples communicate and connect more effectively. For example, guided conversations provide prompts for deeper discussion, as well as short exercises for building intimacy and trust. Mindfulness exercises and meditations are also designed to help users manage stress and anxiety, which can impact relationships.

The app includes a library of articles and videos on topics related to relationships, communication, and self-care, as well as a community forum where users can connect with other couples for support and advice. Users can also track their progress and see how their relationship has improved over time.

One unique feature of Lasting is its focus on small, daily habits that can make a big difference in a relationship. The app encourages users to make small changes and practice new skills daily rather than overwhelming themselves with big, difficult tasks.

The Art and Science of Love by The Gottman Institute

The Art and Science of Love is a mobile app created by The Gottman Institute, a leading relationship research and therapy organization. The app is designed to help couples strengthen their relationship and build deeper emotional connections.

The app includes various features and tools based on the principles of the Gottman Method, a research-based approach to couples therapy developed by Drs. John and Julie Gottman. Some of the key features of the app include:

Love Maps: The Love Maps feature provides questions designed to help couples get to know each other better and build a stronger emotional connection.

Shared Meaning: This feature helps couples identify their shared values, goals, and dreams and work together to create a shared vision for their future.

Conflict Management: The app includes tools for managing conflict and improving communication, including strategies for de-escalating arguments and expressing feelings in a constructive way.

Intimacy and Sex: The app includes exercises and activities designed to enhance intimacy and sexual connection in the relationship.

Mindfulness: The app includes guided meditations and exercises designed to help couples reduce stress and anxiety and be more present and attentive to each other.

Relationship Tips: The app includes a library of articles and tips on topics related to relationships, communication, and self-care.

One of the unique features of The Art and Science of Love app is that it includes video demonstrations of the Gottman Method in action, featuring real couples working through common relationship issues. This allows users to see the principles of the Gottman Method in action and learn how to apply them to their own relationships.

Hold Me Tight Online by Dr. Sue Johnson

Hold Me Tight Online is an online program based on the Hold Me Tight book and workshop by Dr. Sue Johnson, a leading expert in the field of couples therapy and the creator of Emotionally Focused Therapy (EFT). The program is designed to help couples improve their emotional connection, deepen their intimacy, and create a stronger, more fulfilling relationship.

The Hold Me Tight Online program includes a series of videos and exercises that guide couples through the steps of the Hold Me Tight process. The program is divided into seven sessions, each focusing on a different aspect of the relationship:

Recognizing the Demon Dialogues: This session helps couples identify negative communication patterns that can lead to conflict and disconnection.

Finding the Raw Spots: This session helps couples identify their emotional triggers and vulnerabilities and learn how to express them to their partner constructively.

Revisiting a Rocky Moment: This session helps couples work through a specific conflict or difficult moment in their relationship and learn how to communicate more effectively and supportably.

Hold Me Tight: This session focuses on building an emotional connection and intimacy through physical touch and nonverbal communication.

Forgiving Injuries: This session helps couples process past hurts and forgive each other for mistakes and misunderstandings.

Bonding Through Sex and Touch: This session explores the role of physical intimacy in the relationship and helps couples develop a deeper, more fulfilling sexual connection.

Keeping Your Love Alive: This final session provides tools and strategies for maintaining the progress made throughout the program and building a strong, healthy relationship over time.

Throughout the program, couples are encouraged to complete exercises and assignments together and to communicate openly and honestly with each other about their feelings and experiences. The program is designed to be self-paced and can be completed from the comfort of your own home.

WEEK 9: MONEY, MONEY MANAGEMENT, AND FINANCES

Money and finance can play a significant role in a relationship, and managing them effectively is important for the health and longevity of the relationship. Here are some reasons why:

Shared goals: Money is a tool to help couples achieve shared goals, such as buying a home, saving for a vacation, or planning for retirement. When couples are aligned on their financial goals, it can strengthen their connection and sense of partnership.

Communication: Money can be difficult to discuss, and disagreements about finances can cause tension and conflict in a relationship. However, addressing financial issues together can also be an opportunity for couples to practice open and honest communication, which can strengthen their bond.

Trust: Financial transparency and honesty help build trust in a relationship. Being open about your financial situation, including debts and spending habits, can demonstrate a commitment to the relationship and a willingness to work together towards financial stability.

Stress: Financial stress can be a major source of anxiety and strain in a relationship. When couples are able to manage their finances effectively, it can reduce stress and improve overall relationship satisfaction.

Power dynamics: Money can also impact power dynamics in a relationship. When one partner has more financial control or resources, it can create imbalances in the relationship, leading to resentment or conflict. Therefore, it's important for couples to discuss and establish a mutually agreed-upon approach to managing their finances.

In order to manage money and finances in a relationship, couples should establish open and honest communication, set goals, and develop a plan for managing their finances together. This may involve creating a joint budget, setting guidelines for spending and saving, and discussing long-term financial plans. By working together and being transparent about their financial situation, couples can strengthen their relationship and build a foundation for long-term financial stability. Here are the concepts and techniques couples can use to manage their finances.

Understanding the Role of Money in Relationships

The Influence of Personal Beliefs and Values on Money Management

Personal beliefs and values can significantly influence money management in a relationship. Some ways in which personal beliefs and values can shape financial decisions are:

Attitudes towards money: One's beliefs and attitudes towards money can impact how one manages their finances. For example, someone who values frugality may prioritize saving over spending. In contrast, someone who places a high value on experiences may be more willing to spend money on travel or entertainment.

Priorities and goals: Personal beliefs and values can also influence what a person considers to be a priority in their life. For example, someone who values education may prioritize saving for their children's college tuition, while someone who prioritizes social justice may prioritize charitable giving.

Financial decision-making: One's beliefs and values can also shape financial decisions. For example, someone who values independence may be more likely to manage their own finances, while someone who values collaboration may prefer to make financial decisions jointly with their partner.

Risk tolerance: Personal beliefs and values can also influence one's risk tolerance when it comes to investing or taking on debt. For example, someone who values financial security may be more risk-averse, while someone who values entrepreneurship may be more willing to take risks.

When managing finances in a relationship, it's important to be aware of how personal beliefs and values can impact financial decisions. Couples should work to understand each other's values and priorities and to develop a shared approach to managing their finances that reflects both partners' beliefs and values. This may involve compromise, communication, and a willingness to be open-minded and flexible. By understanding and respecting each other's beliefs and values, couples can build a stronger, more cohesive approach to managing their finances and achieving their shared financial goals.

Recognizing the Impact of Financial Stress on Relationships

Financial stress can have a significant impact on relationships, particularly romantic relationships. Money problems can cause tension, arguments, and feelings of insecurity and uncertainty about the future. Some outcomes of how financial stress can affect relationships include:

Communication breakdown: Financial stress can make it difficult for couples to communicate effectively, leading to misunderstandings, arguments, and resentment.

Trust issues: When finances are tight, it can be tempting for one or both partners to hide expenses or make financial decisions without consulting the other. This can erode trust and lead to further relationship problems.

Different spending habits: Couples may have different spending habits or priorities, which can lead to disagreements about how money should be spent.

Power imbalances: In some cases, one partner may be the primary breadwinner, creating power imbalances in the relationship. This imbalance can lead to feelings of resentment or inadequacy on the part of the other partner.

Health problems: Financial stress can also have physical and mental health consequences, which can further strain a relationship.

It's important for couples to recognize the impact of financial stress on their relationship and to work together to manage their finances in a way that works for both partners. It might involve setting shared financial goals, creating a budget, and communicating openly and honestly about money matters. Seeking the help of a financial advisor or couples therapist can also be beneficial.

Exploring Individual Financial Styles

Identifying Each Partner's Money Mindset and Habits

Identifying each partner's money mindset and habits can be valuable for couples who want to understand each other's financial behaviors better and work towards shared financial goals. Here are some steps couples can take to identify their money mindset and habits:

Understand your money mindset: The first step is understanding your beliefs and attitudes towards money. This involves reflecting on your upbringing, cultural background, and personal experiences with money. Consider what money means to you and how your beliefs and attitudes shape your financial behaviors.

Identify your financial habits: Take a close look at your spending and saving habits. Then, look at your bank statements and credit card bills to understand where your money is going. Next, consider how you prioritize spending and whether any patterns or habits contribute to financial stress or conflict in your relationship.

Discuss your partner's money mindset and habits: Once you have a better understanding of your own money mindset and habits, it's important to have a conversation with your partner to understand their perspective. Ask open-ended questions to encourage them to share their thoughts and experiences with money and listen without judgment.

Look for patterns and differences: As you discuss your money mindset and habits, look for patterns and differences between you and your partner. For example, do you have similar attitudes toward money, or are there significant differences? Are there habits causing tension in your relationship or areas where you can work together to achieve shared financial goals?

Develop a plan: Once you have identified your money mindset and habits, and those of your partner, you can develop a plan for managing your finances together. Again, it's important to work together to find a solution that works for both partners and reflects your beliefs and values.

Identifying each partner's money mindset and habits can be a challenging but rewarding process. By working together to understand each other's perspectives and develop a shared approach to managing your finances, you can strengthen your relationship and achieve your financial goals.

Assessing How Individual Financial Styles Can Complement or Clash

Financial styles can complement or clash in a relationship depending on how well they align with each other. Some people are natural savers, while others are risk-averse. These individual financial styles can be either complementary or conflicting.

Complementary financial styles:

Saver and spender: In this scenario, one partner is more inclined to save, while the other is more inclined to spend. When both partners understand and respect each other's financial styles, they can balance each other. The saver can help the spender to prioritize and plan their spending, while the spender can help the saver to loosen up and enjoy life a little.

Risk-taker and risk-averse: One partner may be more comfortable taking risks with money, while the other prefers to play it safe. When both partners work together, they can make informed financial decisions that balance the benefits of taking risks with the need for stability.

Conflicting financial styles:

Tightwad and spender: When one partner is a tightwad and the other is a spender, it can cause friction in the relationship. The tightwad may feel anxious and stressed about every expense, while the spender may feel constrained and frustrated by budgeting constraints.

Competitive savers: Sometimes, both partners may be natural savers, but their approaches to saving money may clash. One partner may want to save aggressively, while the other wants to save more moderately. This can create tension in the relationship, especially if both partners are unwilling to compromise.

To manage conflicting financial styles, couples need open and honest communication about their financial habits, goals, and priorities. They should find common ground and a shared vision for their financial future. Couples can create a financial plan that works for both partners by working together and compromising where necessary.

Gottman's Approach to Financial Management in Relationships

Establishing Shared Financial Goals and Values

The Gottman Method for Couples Therapy emphasizes the importance of establishing shared financial goals and values as a key component of building a strong and healthy relationship. Here are some steps that couples can take to establish shared financial goals and values, according to the Gottman Method:

Have a conversation about your financial goals: Sit down together and have an open and honest conversation about your financial goals. Discuss what you want to achieve financially in the short-term and long-term and what steps you need to take to get there.

Identify your shared values: Talk about your shared values regarding money, such as the importance of financial security, freedom, or generosity. Identify the most important values to both of you and use them to guide your financial decisions.

Create a budget together: Work together to create a budget that reflects your shared financial goals and values. Identify your monthly expenses, prioritize your spending, and set aside money for savings and investments.

Set financial boundaries: Talk about your individual spending habits and agree on financial boundaries that you are both comfortable with. This may involve setting limits on discretionary spending or agreeing on a joint bank account.

Regularly check in and adjust your plan: As your financial situation changes, check in regularly to ensure that you are staying on track with your goals and values. Then, adjust your plan as needed to reflect changes in your income, expenses, or priorities.

Creating a "financial love map"

A "financial love map" is a tool that couples can use to gain a better understanding of each other's financial values, goals, and habits. It involves creating a shared vision for the future of the couple's finances and developing a plan to achieve it. Here are the steps to creating a financial love map:

Discuss financial history and values: Each partner should share their financial history, upbringing, and any significant financial experiences. This will help to identify any differences in financial values and beliefs.

Identify financial goals: Both partners should identify their financial goals, such as paying off debt, saving for a down payment on a house, or retirement.

Develop a budget: Create a budget that reflects both partners' financial goals and values. This should include tracking income and expenses, setting spending limits, and creating a plan to pay off debt.

Determine financial roles and responsibilities: Decide who will manage certain aspects of the finances, such as paying bills, investing, or tracking expenses. It's important to ensure both partners feel involved and empowered in financial decision-making.

Establish communication strategies: Regularly check in with each other about finances to ensure that both partners are on the same page.

Implementing regular "money talks"

Regular "money talks" can effectively improve financial literacy, make better financial decisions, and improve financial well-being. These are some steps to implement regular "money talks":

Schedule regular money talks: Set a regular schedule for money talks, such as once a month or once a quarter. Consistency is key to building good habits.

Prepare an agenda: Before the money talk, create an agenda of topics to discuss. This could include reviewing budgets, setting financial goals, discussing investments, or reviewing bills and expenses.

Track progress: Keep track of progress and follow up on action items from previous money talks. Celebrate successes and address any challenges that arise.

Make it fun: Money talks don't have to be boring or stressful. Make them fun by including games, incentives, or rewards for meeting financial goals.

Remember, regular money talks aim to improve financial literacy and make better financial decisions.

EFT's perspective on money and attachment

Recognizing the emotional aspects of financial decision

Financial decisions are not always rational and logical. Emotions can significantly affect how we approach money and make financial decisions. Recognizing the emotional aspects of financial decisions is important because it can help us make better financial choices and reduce money-related stress and anxiety. Here are some steps to recognize the emotional aspects of financial decisions:

Identify your emotions: Before making a financial decision, take a moment to identify your emotions. Understanding your emotions can help you recognize how they may affect your decision-making process.

Acknowledge your biases: We all have biases that affect how we approach money. For example, we may have a fear of missing out (FOMO) or a desire to keep up with others. Acknowledging these biases can help you make more informed decisions.

Consider the impact on your relationships: Money can have a significant impact on our relationships with others. Consider how your financial decisions may affect your relationships with your partner, family, or friends.

Seek support: If you are struggling with making a financial decision or managing your emotions related to money, seek support from a financial advisor, therapist, or trusted friend or family member.

Recognizing the emotional aspects of financial decisions can help you make more informed choices, reduce stress and anxiety related to money, and improve your overall financial well-being.

How attachment styles may influence money management

Attachment styles can influence how individuals approach money management, both in their finances and in their relationships. Attachment styles are patterns of behavior and beliefs that form in childhood and affect how individuals form relationships in adulthood. There are four primary attachment styles:

Secure attachment: Individuals with a secure attachment style tend to be comfortable with intimacy and are generally trusting in relationships. This translates into a healthy attitude towards money management, where they are comfortable with financial planning, can communicate openly about financial matters, and make joint decisions with their partner.

Anxious attachment: Individuals with an anxious attachment style tend to be more insecure and fear abandonment. This can lead to a more cautious approach to money management, where they may be more prone to saving and avoiding risks. They may also be more likely to worry about financial stability and have difficulty making financial decisions with their partner.

Avoidant attachment: Individuals with an avoidant attachment style tend to prefer individual financial planning and decision-making rather than joint planning with a partner.

Fearful-avoidant attachment: Individuals with a fearful-avoidant attachment style tend to avoid financial planning and decision-making altogether, leading to financial difficulties and instability.

Understanding your attachment style can help you recognize tendencies toward certain financial behaviors and beliefs. By recognizing these tendencies and working to address them, individuals can develop healthier financial habits and build stronger relationships.

Addressing Financial Fears and Insecurities Together

Addressing financial fears and insecurities can help improve the financial well-being and strengthen relationships. Here are some steps to address financial fears and insecurities together:

Create a safe space for discussion: Creating a safe and non-judgmental space for discussion is essential to address financial fears and insecurities together. Avoid blaming or criticizing each other, and focus on listening and understanding each other's perspectives.

Identify your financial fears and insecurities: Take some time to identify your financial fears and insecurities. For example, are you worried about debt, losing your job, or not having enough money for retirement? Understanding your fears and insecurities can help you communicate them to your partner or family.

Develop a plan: Once you have identified your financial fears and insecurities, develop a plan to achieve your financial goals. Consider seeking advice from a financial advisor or counselor if necessary.

Hold each other accountable: Holding each other accountable can help you stay on track with your financial goals. Regular check-ins and communication can help you stay motivated and keep on track.

Celebrate successes: Celebrating successes, no matter how small, can help reinforce positive financial habits and strengthen your relationship.

Addressing financial fears and insecurities together requires open communication, empathy, and a willingness to work together toward common goals. By creating a safe space for discussion, you can overcome financial fears and insecurities together and improve your overall financial well-being.

Exercises and activities for effective financial management

The "Money Autobiography"

The "Money Autobiography" tool can help individuals reflect on their relationship with money and better understand their financial values, beliefs, and behaviors. Here are some steps to create a "Money Autobiography":

Start with your earliest memories of money: Think back to your earliest memories. What did money represent to you? How did you feel about money?

Reflect on your upbringing: How did your upbringing and family influence your relationship with money? Did your parents or guardians teach you about money? How did they handle money?

Consider significant financial events: Reflect on significant financial events in your life, such as your first job, major purchases, or financial setbacks. How did these events shape your relationship with money?

Identify your financial values and beliefs: Consider your financial values and beliefs. What is important to you when it comes to money? What are your priorities?

Examine your financial habits: Take a closer look at your financial habits. Do they align with your financial values and beliefs? Are there any habits that you would like to change?

Set financial goals: Based on your reflection and examination of your financial values, beliefs, and habits, set financial goals that align with your priorities.

Creating a "Money Autobiography" can help you better understand your relationship with money and identify areas for improvement. It can also help you set financial goals that align with your values and priorities.

Setting short-term and long-term financial goals together

Setting short-term and long-term financial goals can help couples or families work towards a common financial vision and improve their overall financial well-being. Some steps to set short-term and long-term financial goals together are:

Identify your shared financial vision: It is important to identify your vision before setting financial goals. What do you want to achieve with your money in the short and long term? What are your financial priorities?

Break down your financial vision into short-term and long-term goals: Once you have identified your shared financial vision, break it down into short-term and long-term goals. Short-term goals can usually be achieved within a year or less, while long-term goals take longer to achieve, such as saving for retirement or a down payment on a home.

Make your goals SMART: SMART stands for Specific, Measurable, Achievable, Relevant, and Time-bound. Make sure your goals meet all these criteria. For example, instead of setting a goal to "save money," set a goal to "save $5,000 for a down payment on a house by December 31, 2023."

Prioritize your goals: Prioritize your goals based on your shared financial vision and your current financial situation. Consider which goals are most important and which ones can be deferred.

Develop a plan to achieve your goals: Once you have identified your short-term and long-term goals, develop a plan to achieve them.

Track your progress and make adjustments: Regularly track your progress and make adjustments as needed. And remember to celebrate successes and learn from setbacks.

By identifying your shared financial vision, breaking it down into SMART goals, prioritizing your goals, developing a plan to achieve them, and tracking your progress, you can achieve financial success together.

Creating a Joint Budget and Financial Plan

Creating a joint budget and financial plan is important to achieving financial success as a couple or family. Some steps to create a joint budget and financial plan are:

Identify your income: Determine your combined income from all sources, including employment, investments, and any other sources.

Determine your expenses: Track your expenses over the past several months to get an idea of your average monthly expenses. Then, categorize your expenses into fixed expenses (such as rent or mortgage payments) and variable expenses (such as groceries or entertainment).

Create a budget: Create a budget that reflects your income, expenses, and financial goals. Allocate your income to cover your fixed expenses first, then assign a portion to your variable expenses and financial goals.

Consider debt repayment: If you have debt, consider including a repayment plan in your budget. Prioritize high-interest debt, such as credit card debt, and consider consolidating or refinancing if it will help you save money.

Review and adjust regularly: Review your budget regularly to track your progress towards your financial goals and adjust your budget as needed.

Consider working with a financial advisor: If you need help creating a joint budget and financial plan or need guidance on achieving your financial goals, consider working with a financial advisor.

Creating a joint budget and financial plan can help you and your partner or family work towards a common financial vision and improve your overall financial well-being.

Financial check-ins

Financial check-ins are important for couples to ensure they stay on track with their financial goals and to address any issues that may arise. Here are some tips for conducting regular financial check-ins:

Set a schedule: Establish a regular schedule for financial check-ins, such as once a month or once every few months. This will help ensure you remember to review your finances and make any necessary adjustments.

Review your budget: Look at your budget and ensure that you are sticking to it. If there are any areas where you could be spending more, make adjustments to your budget.

Plan for upcoming expenses: Review any upcoming expenses and determine how they will be paid for. If necessary, adjust your budget to accommodate these expenses.

Check credit reports: Regularly review your credit reports to ensure that there are no errors or fraudulent activity. This can help you to maintain good credit and avoid financial problems down the line.

By conducting regular financial check-ins, couples can ensure that they stay on track with their financial goals and communicate effectively about their finances. This helps avoid conflicts and build a stronger financial foundation for the future.

Useful resources for managing money and finances in relationships

Books:

"Smart Couples Finish Rich" by David Bach

"Smart Couples Finish Rich" by David Bach is a personal finance book that provides couples with strategies to manage their money and build wealth together. The book covers a range of topics, including creating a joint financial plan, managing debt, investing, and saving for retirement.

Bach emphasizes the importance of communication and shared goals in managing finances as a couple. He encourages couples to establish a clear vision of their financial future and work together to achieve their goals.

The book provides practical advice on how to save money, including setting up automatic savings plans, tracking expenses, and reducing unnecessary expenses. It also covers strategies for managing debt, including credit card debt, student loans, and mortgages.

Bach also emphasizes the importance of investing for the future and provides guidance on how to build a diversified investment portfolio that aligns with the couple's financial goals and risk tolerance.

"The 5 Money Conversations to Have with Your Kids at Every Age and Stage" by Scott and Bethany Palmer

"The 5 Money Conversations to Have with Your Kids at Every Age and Stage" by Scott and Bethany Palmer is a book that offers practical advice and strategies for teaching children about money management at different stages of their lives.

The book is organized around five key money conversations that parents should have with their children:

The Value of Work: This conversation focuses on teaching children about the importance of work and helping them develop a strong work ethic.

Spending and Saving: In this conversation, Parents are encouraged to help their children set savings goals, create a budget, and involve them in family financial decisions.

Giving: This conversation focuses on teaching children the importance of giving back and helping others.

Debt: Parents in this part of the book are encouraged to help their children understand the consequences of borrowing and to teach them about responsible credit use.

Investing: This conversation is about teaching children about investing and building wealth for the future.

Overall, the book emphasizes the importance of starting early, involving children in family financial decisions, and teaching them about responsible money management at every stage.

Podcasts:

"The Money Couple" by Scott and Bethany Palmer

"The Money Couple" is a podcast hosted by Scott and Bethany Palmer, a husband and wife team who are financial advisors and authors of the book "The 5 Money Conversations to Have with Your Kids at Every Age and Stage."

On the podcast, Scott and Bethany discuss various topics related to money management and relationships, including budgeting, saving, investing, and retirement planning. They also provide practical tips and strategies for couples and families to improve their financial health and communication.

In addition, the podcast features interviews with experts in personal finance and relationships, as well as real-life stories from couples who have overcome financial challenges and achieved financial success together.

"The Smart Money Show" by David Bach

"The Smart Money Show" is a podcast hosted by David Bach, the author of several personal finance books, including "Smart Women Finish Rich" and "The Automatic Millionaire." In the podcast, Bach discusses various personal finance topics and provides practical advice for listeners to manage their money more effectively.

The podcast is geared toward individuals looking to improve their financial literacy and take control of their finances. Bach emphasizes the importance of taking action and making small changes to improve one's financial situation rather than waiting for a windfall or a significant change in circumstances.

Apps:

Mint

The Mint app is a free personal finance app that allows users to manage their money and track their finances in one place. The app is available on both iOS and Android devices.

Here are some of the features of the Mint app:

Budgeting: The Mint app allows users to create a budget and track their expenses against it. The app categorizes transactions automatically and provides users with alerts when they go over budget in a particular category.

Bill-tracking: The app allows users to track their bills and get reminders when they are due. Users can also set up automatic payments for bills.

Credit score monitoring: Mint offers users free access to their credit score, along with personalized tips for improving it.

Investment tracking: The app allows users to track their investment accounts, including 401(k)s, IRAs, and brokerage accounts.

You Need a Budget (YNAB)

You Need a Budget, commonly referred to as YNAB, is a popular budgeting app that helps users gain control of their finances and achieve their financial goals. The app is available for web, iOS, and Android devices.

At its core, YNAB is based on the principle of zero-based budgeting, which means that every dollar you earn is assigned a specific job, such as paying bills, saving for a future expense, or investing for retirement. As a result, YNAB helps you track your income and expenses and provides a clear picture of where your money is going each month.

Some key features of the YNAB app include:

Goal setting: YNAB allows you to set financial goals. Also, You can track your progress toward your goals and adjust your budget as needed.

Automatic syncing: YNAB automatically syncs with your bank accounts and credit cards, so you can easily track your transactions and reconcile your accounts.

Budget categories: YNAB allows you to create custom budget categories based on your spending habits and provides helpful suggestions for categories you might have yet to consider.

Financial Peace University by Dave Ramsey

Financial Peace University (FPU) is a nine-week personal finance course created by Dave Ramsey, a financial expert, and author. The course aims to teach individuals and couples the principles of personal finance and provide them with the tools they need to manage their money effectively. Also, The course is available both in-person and online, making it accessible to a wide range of individuals and couples.

Here are some of the key components of the Financial Peace University course:

Budgeting: The course teaches participants how to create a budget that works for them and their lifestyle.

Debt reduction: The course provides strategies for paying off debt, including the "debt snowball" method, which involves paying off the smallest debt first and then moving on to the next smallest debt.

Savings: The course emphasizes the importance of building an emergency fund and saving for long-term goals such as retirement and children's college education.

Investing: The course covers the basics of investing and provides participants with information on how to build a diversified investment portfolio.

Insurance: The course provides guidance on selecting insurance policies, including health insurance, life insurance, and auto insurance.

Estate planning: The course covers the basics of estate planning, including creating a will and establishing a trust.

Money Harmony Workshops for Couples by Olivia Mellan and Sherry Christie

Money Harmony Workshops for Couples is a program developed by financial therapists Olivia Mellan and Sherry Christie. The program is designed to help couples improve their communication around money and develop a shared approach to managing their finances.

It is a series of exercises and activities designed to help couples explore their money personalities, values, and beliefs about money. The program emphasizes the importance of open communication and mutual respect in managing money as a couple.

Some of the key components of the Money Harmony Workshops for Couples program include:

Identifying your money personality: The program helps couples identify their unique money personalities and understand how they may affect their money management approach.

Exploring values and beliefs: The program helps couples explore their values and beliefs about money and then work together to develop shared values and goals around money.

Creating a shared financial plan: The program helps couples develop a shared financial plan that reflects their shared values and goals around money.

Overall, Money Harmony Workshops for Couples is a useful program for couples who are looking to improve their communication around money and develop a shared approach to managing their finances.

Finances and money can play a significant role in the success or failure of a couple's relationship. Therefore, understanding their function and importance in a relationship is essential to building a strong, healthy, and long-lasting partnership.

Money can reflect shared values, beliefs, and goals. How a couple manages their finances can reveal their priorities, such as valuing experiences or material possessions or prioritizing short-term gratification over long-term stability. This can help identify areas of compatibility or potential conflict, which helps the couple achieve their goals in the long run.

WEEK 10: SUPPORTING INDIVIDUAL GROWTH

When you support individual growth in a relationship, you encourage and facilitate your partner's personal development while also pursuing your own growth and development.

This can involve a variety of actions, such as:

- Encouraging your partner to pursue their interests and passions, even if they differ from yours.
- Being supportive of your partner's personal goals and aspirations and helping them to achieve those goals.
- Being open to constructive criticism and feedback and using it to improve your personal growth and development.
- Respecting each other's individuality and autonomy and not trying to control or change your partner.

By supporting individual growth in a relationship, you can build a stronger foundation for your partnership based on mutual respect, trust, and support for each other's growth and development.

THE IMPORTANCE OF PERSONAL GROWTH IN A RELATIONSHIP

FOSTERING A SENSE OF AUTONOMY AND INDEPENDENCE

Fostering a sense of autonomy and independence is crucial for healthy relationships, whether it's a romantic partnership, friendship, or family relationship. When individuals feel they have the freedom to be themselves and pursue their goals and interests, it can lead to greater personal fulfillment and stronger and more resilient relationships.

Here are some ways to foster a sense of autonomy and independence in relationships:

Encourage individual passions and pursuits: It's important to support and encourage each other's interests and hobbies, even if they don't align. Encouraging each other to pursue individual passions can lead to personal growth and fulfillment, ultimately benefiting the relationship.

Respect each other's boundaries: Respecting each other's boundaries is crucial for fostering a sense of autonomy and independence. This means respecting each other's physical and emotional space and not trying to control or change the other person. It's important to communicate openly and honestly about boundaries and to work together to establish boundaries that feel comfortable for both partners.

Share responsibilities equally: Sharing responsibilities equally is an important aspect of fostering autonomy and independence in a relationship. This means dividing household chores, financial responsibilities, and other tasks fairly so each partner can pursue their goals and interests.

Embrace individual differences: Embracing individual differences is another key aspect of fostering autonomy and independence in a relationship. This means accepting and celebrating each other's unique qualities and strengths rather than trying to change or mold the other person to fit your expectations.

Take time for self-care: Self-care fosters autonomy and independence in a relationship. It means prioritizing activities that promote personal well-being, such as exercise, meditation, or spending time alone. It's important to communicate openly with your partner about your need for self-care and to support each other's efforts to prioritize self-care.

Overall, fostering a sense of autonomy and independence in relationships is essential for promoting personal growth and fulfillment, as well as building strong and resilient partnerships.

Encouraging self-discovery and self-improvement

Encouraging self-discovery and self-improvement is essential for personal growth and also benefits relationships in various ways.

Some ways to encourage self-discovery and self-improvement in relationships are:

Create a safe and supportive environment: It's important to create an atmosphere where partners feel comfortable expressing themselves and exploring their thoughts and feelings. Partners should feel free to be vulnerable without fear of judgment or criticism.

Encourage self-reflection: Encourage your partner to reflect on their thoughts, emotions, and behaviors. This can help them gain greater self-awareness and insight into their needs and desires.

Provide constructive feedback: Providing constructive feedback can help your partner identify areas for self-improvement. However, it's important to provide feedback in a way that is supportive and non-judgmental, focusing on the behavior rather than the person.

Celebrate small victories: Recognizing and celebrating small accomplishments can motivate and help your partner stay focused on their personal growth and keep progressing toward their goals.

Share resources: Sharing resources such as books, articles, podcasts, and workshops that align with your partner's interests and goals can help them to explore new ideas and gain new skills.

Be a supportive accountability partner: This tip entails Checking in with your partner regularly to see how they're doing and offer support and encouragement as needed. You can also set goals together and hold each other accountable for progress.

By practicing these tips in day-to-day life, couples can support and encourage each other's personal growth and development, leading to a deeper and more fulfilling relationship.

Recognizing the Benefits of Individual Growth for Relationship Health

When partners are committed to their personal growth and development, it can lead to increased emotional intelligence, greater self-awareness, and improved communication skills. The benefits of individual growth for relationship health include:

Improved communication: When partners have a better understanding of themselves and their own needs, they are better able to communicate those needs to their partner. This can lead to more effective communication, fewer misunderstandings, and a stronger and more resilient relationship.

Increased emotional intelligence: Personal growth can lead to increased emotional intelligence, which is the ability to recognize and manage one's own emotions, as well as the emotions of others. When partners have a higher level of emotional intelligence, they can empathize with each other, understand each other's perspective, and work through challenges together.

Greater self-awareness: Self-awareness is understanding one's thoughts, feelings, and behaviors. When partners have a better understanding of themselves, they are better able to communicate their needs and boundaries to their partners, which can lead to greater trust, respect, and intimacy in the relationship.

Enhanced problem-solving skills: Personal growth can also lead to enhanced problem-solving skills, which are essential for healthy relationships. When partners are committed to their personal growth, they can approach problems with a more open and flexible mindset and find mutually beneficial solutions.

Increased confidence: When partners are confident in themselves and their abilities, they are more likely to communicate their needs and boundaries to their partner. As a result, this leads to greater trust, respect, and intimacy in the relationship.

Greater independence: Personal growth can also lead to greater independence. Partners who are committed to personal growth can pursue their interests and goals independently.

Overall, individual growth can have numerous benefits for relationship health, leading to a deeper and more fulfilling relationship.

Encouraging each other's dreams and aspirations

Encouraging each other's dreams and aspirations is important to supporting individual growth in a relationship. Partners supporting each other's goals and aspirations can lead to greater happiness, fulfillment, and personal growth.

Understanding the role of support and encouragement in achieving personal goals

Support and encouragement play a crucial role in achieving personal goals. The benefits include:

1. Increased motivation: When someone feels supported and encouraged, it can increase their motivation to pursue their goals. Knowing someone believes in them and cheers them on can be incredibly motivating.
2. Enhanced self-confidence: When someone has people who believe in them and support their goals, it can boost their confidence and help them overcome self-doubt.
3. Accountability: When someone has a support system, they are more likely to stay committed to their goals and follow through on their plans.
4. Celebrating successes: Celebrating successes can help reinforce positive behavior and motivate someone to continue pursuing their goals.

Ultimately, support and encouragement are essential for achieving personal goals. Whether pursuing a career change, starting a new hobby, or working towards a fitness goal, having people in one's corner can make all the difference.

Creating a safe environment for sharing ambitions and dreams

Creating a safe environment for sharing ambitions and dreams is essential for supporting individual growth in a relationship. You can create a safe environment by applying some techniques, which include:

Practice active listening: Active listening involves paying full attention to what the other person is saying, asking clarifying questions, and reflecting on what was said. When someone feels that they are being actively listened to, they are more likely to feel heard and understood.

Show empathy: Empathy involves putting oneself in another person's shoes and trying to understand their perspective. When someone feels that their partner is empathetic towards them, they are more likely to feel validated and understood.

Avoid judgment: It's important to avoid judging the other person's goals and dreams, even if they seem unrealistic or difficult to achieve. Instead, focus on being supportive and encouraging.

Be open-minded: Being open-minded involves considering new ideas and perspectives, even if they differ from one's own. When someone feels that their partner is open-minded towards their goals and aspirations, they are more likely to feel comfortable sharing them.

Provide constructive feedback: Providing constructive feedback involves offering feedback in a supportive and helpful way. When someone receives constructive feedback, they are more likely to feel that their partner is invested in their growth and development.

Celebrate successes: Celebrating successes can help reinforce positive behavior and motivate someone to continue pursuing their goals.

Creating a safe environment for sharing ambitions and dreams requires trust, open communication, and a willingness to be vulnerable. By practicing open communication, partners can create a safe and supportive environment for each other's growth and development.

Establishing regular check-ins to discuss and review personal goals

Establishing regular check-ins to discuss and review personal goals is a great way to support individual growth in a relationship. Here are some tips for establishing regular check-ins:

1. Set a schedule: It's important to set a regular schedule for check-ins, such as weekly or monthly. This helps to ensure that the check-ins are a regular part of the relationship and that both partners are committed to making them happen.
2. Create an agenda: Before each check-in, create an agenda to discuss the personal goals that each partner has set and the progress made towards achieving them.
3. Be supportive: When discussing personal goals, being supportive and encouraging is important. Ask questions to understand the other person's goals and offer suggestions or resources to help them achieve them.
4. Celebrate successes: Celebrate successes along the way, no matter how small they may be. Recognizing progress can reinforce positive behavior and motivate someone to pursue their goals.

5. Offer feedback: Provide support and encouragement while helping the other person identify improvement areas.
6. Adjust goals as needed: As personal circumstances change, it may be necessary to adjust personal goals. And remember to provide support during the adjustment process.

Regular check-ins ensure that both partners are aware of each other's personal goals and actively support each other's growth and development. By following the previous tips, partners can work together to achieve personal goals and strengthen relationships.

EFT's Concept of Differentiation and Interdependence

Emotion-focused therapy (EFT) is a form of couples therapy that focuses on the emotional bonds between partners. EFT emphasizes the importance of differentiation and interdependence in a relationship and how they can support healthy emotional bonds.

Differentiation refers to the ability of each partner to maintain a separate sense of self while still being emotionally connected to their partner. It involves balancing the needs for both independence and connection in a relationship. EFT emphasizes how differentiation allows partners to maintain their identities while being emotionally close to each other.

Interdependence, on the other hand, refers to the emotional connection between partners. Interdependence is necessary for emotional bonding, as it involves sharing emotions, thoughts, and experiences with each other.

EFT views differentiation and interdependence as two sides of the same coin, both necessary for a healthy relationship. For example, when partners are too emotionally fused, they may lose their sense of self and become overly dependent on each other. This can lead to anxiety, depression, and a lack of fulfillment in the relationship. On the other hand, when partners are too emotionally distant, they may become disconnected from each other and lose the emotional bond that is necessary for a healthy relationship.

EFT seeks to help couples find a balance between differentiation and interdependence by promoting open communication, emotional expression, and empathy.

Balancing the need for individual growth with the desire for emotional closeness

Balancing the need for individual growth with the desire for emotional closeness is essential for a healthy and fulfilling relationship. On the one hand, each partner in a relationship has their own unique goals, aspirations, and personal growth needs. Yet, on the other hand, both partners need emotional closeness, connection, and intimacy to feel secure and fulfilled in the relationship.

To balance these needs, partners must communicate openly and honestly about their goals, needs, and desires. This requires a willingness to listen to each other without judgment and to show empathy and understanding.

When partners feel supported and encouraged in their individual pursuits, they are likely to feel more fulfilled and satisfied in the relationship. This, in turn, can lead to a deeper emotional bond between partners.

To balance the need for individual growth with the desire for emotional closeness, partners can take the following steps:

1. Communicate openly: Discuss personal goals and desires with each other, and listen to each other's perspectives with an open mind.
2. Show support: Encourage each other to pursue personal goals and support each other's efforts to grow and develop.
3. Create shared goals: Identify areas where you can work together to achieve shared goals and support each other's efforts toward those goals.
4. Make time for each other: Despite busy schedules and individual pursuits, make time for each other regularly. It could be through date nights or other shared activities that promote emotional closeness.
5. Show appreciation: Express gratitude for each other's efforts to grow and support each other. Showing appreciation can strengthen the emotional bond between partners.

In summary, balancing individual growth with the desire for emotional closeness requires open communication, support, and a willingness to work together towards shared goals. By showing empathy, understanding, and appreciation for each other's efforts, partners can build a strong emotional bond while still pursuing their individual goals and aspirations.

Developing a healthy sense of self while maintaining a strong connection with your partner

Developing a healthy sense of self while maintaining a strong connection with your partner is key to a healthy and fulfilling relationship. It involves striking a balance between independence and interdependence, or the ability to maintain your identity while being emotionally connected to your partner.

To develop a healthy sense of self, it is important to:

1. Prioritize self-care: Taking care of your physical, emotional, and mental health is essential for developing a healthy sense of self. This includes eating well, exercising regularly, getting enough sleep, and engaging in activities that bring you joy.
2. Set boundaries: Establishing healthy boundaries with your partner can help you maintain your sense of self while being emotionally connected. This involves communicating your needs and limits and respecting each other's boundaries.
3. Practice self-reflection: Self-reflection can help you better understand your thoughts, feelings, and behaviors. This can lead to greater self-awareness and help you develop a stronger sense of self.
4. Pursue personal interests: Pursuing personal interests and hobbies can help you develop a sense of identity separate from your relationship. This can also bring new experiences and perspectives to your relationship.
5. Seek support: Seeking support from friends, family, or a therapist can help you develop a healthy sense of self and maintain emotional balance.

To maintain a strong connection with your partner while developing a healthy sense of self, it is important to:

1. Communicate openly: Open and honest communication is essential for maintaining emotional closeness with your partner. This involves sharing your thoughts, feelings, and experiences without judgment.
2. Show empathy: Demonstrating empathy and understanding toward your partner's feelings and experiences can help strengthen your emotional connection.
3. Be present: Being present and engaged in your relationship can help maintain emotional closeness and strengthen your connection.

4. Practice forgiveness: Forgiving your partner for mistakes or misunderstandings can help prevent resentment and maintain emotional closeness.
5. Show appreciation: Expressing gratitude and appreciation for your partner can help maintain emotional closeness and strengthen your emotional bond.

In summary, striking a balance between independence and interdependence help partners build a healthy and fulfilling relationship that supports personal growth and emotional closeness.

Recognizing the Value of Personal Interests and Activities Outside of the Relationship

Engaging in hobbies and activities that are meaningful and enjoyable to you can help you develop a sense of identity that is separate from your relationship, which in turn can help you maintain a healthy sense of self and prevent feelings of codependency.

Personal interests and activities can also provide a sense of fulfillment and satisfaction that may not be attainable through the relationship alone. Pursuing your interests can give you a sense of accomplishment, mastery, and purpose, improving your overall well-being and happiness.

Additionally, personal interests and activities provide a break from the routine and stress of daily life, which helps reduce stress and promote relaxation. Taking time for yourself and engaging in activities you enjoy can also help you feel recharged and energized, which can benefit both you and your relationship.

Recognizing the value of personal interests and activities also involves respecting and supporting your partner's pursuits. Encouraging your partner to pursue their interests and hobbies can help them develop a healthy sense of self and prevent feelings of resentment or frustration.

However, it is important to strike a balance between pursuing personal interests and maintaining emotional closeness with your partner. Engaging in personal interests and activities should not come at the expense of neglecting your relationship or partner.

In summary, recognizing the value of personal interests and activities outside the relationship is essential for maintaining a healthy and fulfilling relationship. Pursuing interests can help you develop a sense of identity, provide fulfillment, and reduce stress. Supporting your partner's pursuits is also important for a healthy sense of self and preventing resentment or frustration.

ACTIVITIES TO PROMOTE INDIVIDUAL GROWTH AND SELF-CARE

PERSONAL GOAL-SETTING EXERCISE

Setting goals in a relationship is important because it helps partners stay focused on what they want to achieve together and provides a sense of direction and purpose.

Here is a simple personal goal-setting exercise that you can try:

1. Identify your overall goal: Start by identifying a specific area of your life that you want to improve, such as your career, health, relationships, or personal growth. Be as specific as possible and write down your goal.
2. Break it down into smaller goals: Once you have identified your overall goal, break it down into smaller, more manageable goals. For example, if your overall goal is to improve your health, your smaller goals could include exercising three times a week, eating more vegetables, and reducing sugar intake.
3. Create a plan: Once you have identified your smaller goals, create a plan to achieve them. Write down specific actions you will take to achieve each goal, such as running after work, meal planning on Sundays, or taking a cooking class.
4. Set deadlines: Setting deadlines can help you stay accountable and motivated. Assign specific deadlines to each of your goals and actions.
5. Review and adjust: Regularly review your progress and plan as needed. Celebrate your successes and learn from your setbacks.

Remember to be realistic and specific with your goals and actions. Remember to take into consideration your current resources, limitations, and priorities. The goal-setting exercise can be an excellent way to motivate yourself and make progress toward achieving your personal goals.

THE "SUPPORT CIRCLE"

The "Support Circle" activity is a simple yet powerful exercise that can help you identify the people who support you and the types of support you need.

These are the steps for the activity:

1. Draw a large circle on a paper or whiteboard.

2. Write your name in the center of the circle.
3. Think about the people in your life who support you. These could be family members, friends, co-workers, mentors, or anyone you feel supports you. Write their names around the outside of the circle.
4. Next, categorize the types of support that each person provides. For example, one person may be a good listener, another can be someone you turn to for advice, and another may be someone who helps you with practical tasks. Write these categories next to each person's name.
5. Assess the strength of each connection and the type of support they provide. This will help you determine who you can rely on for different types of support.
6. Make a plan: Based on your assessment, make a plan for reaching out to your support network. First, consider who you can turn to for emotional support, practical help, or advice. Then, make a list of specific actions you can take to strengthen these connections.

By completing this activity, you will better understand your support network and the types of support you need. This can help you build stronger connections with those who support you and reach out for help when needed.

Self-care activities

Encouraging each partner to engage in self-care activities is important to maintaining a healthy and happy relationship.

Here are some ideas for self-care activities that can promote physical, emotional, and mental well-being:

1. Exercise: Regular physical exercise can help to reduce stress, improve mood, and increase energy levels. Encourage each other to engage in physical activities that you enjoy, such as going for a walk, practicing yoga, or hitting the gym.
2. Mindfulness: Practicing mindfulness can help to reduce stress and promote emotional well-being. Encourage each other to try meditation, deep breathing exercises, or other relaxation techniques.
3. Creative pursuits: Engaging in creative pursuits can greatly promote mental well-being and reduce stress. Encourage each other to pursue hobbies and interests that you enjoy, such as painting, playing music, or writing.
4. Self-reflection: Taking time for self-reflection can help to promote emotional well-being and personal growth. Encourage each other to journal or engage in self-reflection exercises.

5. Socializing: Spending time with friends and family can help to promote emotional well-being and reduce stress. Encourage each other to make time for socializing and connecting with others.
6. Self-care rituals: Encourage each other to establish self-care rituals, such as taking a relaxing bath, getting a massage, or treating yourself to a favorite meal or snack.

Encouraging each other to engage in self-care activities can help to promote physical, emotional, and mental well-being. It can also help to strengthen your relationship by showing support for each other's personal growth and well-being.

Creating a Culture of Continuous Learning and Growth

Creating a continuous learning and growth culture in a relationship can lead to greater personal fulfillment and satisfaction.

Here are some ways to encourage continuous learning and growth in your relationship:

1. Make a commitment to learning: Set a shared goal with your partner to learn something new each week, whether it's trying a new recipe, taking a class, or reading a book.
2. Encourage each other's interests: Show interest in each other's hobbies and interests, and encourage each other to pursue them.
3. Seek out new experiences together: Try new activities or visit new places together. This can help you to discover new things about each other and create shared memories.
4. Learn from each other: Share your knowledge and skills with each other. This can build mutual respect and deepen your connection.
5. Attend workshops or seminars: Attend workshops or seminars together on topics that interest you. This can provide opportunities to learn and grow as a couple.
6. Celebrate achievements: Celebrate each other's achievements and successes, no matter how small. This helps reinforce the importance of growth and learning in your relationship.
7. Embrace challenges: Encourage each other to embrace challenges and take risks. This can help to build resilience and confidence.

Creating a culture of continuous learning and growth in your relationship can help you to build a strong foundation for personal fulfillment and relationship satisfaction. By encouraging each other to pursue new experiences and interests, you can deepen your connection and support each other's personal growth. Here are other important ways to do so:

Sharing personal interests and hobbies

Sharing personal interests and hobbies with your partner can be a great way to build a stronger connection and add more joy to your relationship. Talking to your partner about what you love to do and why it's important to you can help your partner understand you better and appreciate your interests.

Being open and supportive of each other's interests can deepen your bond and create a more fulfilling relationship.

Setting aside time for individual pursuits and activities

In a healthy relationship, balancing time spent together and pursuing individual interests and activities is important. Here are some tips for setting aside time for individual pursuits and activities:

1. Schedule regular "me time": Schedule regular blocks for each partner to pursue their interests and activities. This could be a few hours every week or a whole day once a month.
2. Respect each other's time: When your partner is engaging in their activities, respect their time and avoid interrupting them unless it's an emergency.
3. Communicate your needs: Communicate your needs and boundaries with your partner. For example, if you need more time for your pursuits, let your partner know in a kind and respectful way.
4. Support each other's goals: Encourage and support each other's goals and aspirations, whether taking up a new hobby, starting a side business, or pursuing a new career.
5. Use technology mindfully: Be mindful of how technology affects your ability to have quality time alone. While getting sucked into social media or emails is easy, it's important to unplug and disconnect from technology during your time.
6. Make time for shared interests: Remember to make time for shared interests and activities. Spending time together and engaging in shared activities can strengthen your relationship and deepen your bond.

Setting aside time for individual pursuits and activities allows you to maintain a healthy sense of self while nurturing your relationship. In addition, this can help prevent resentment or suffocation when partners feel like they don't have enough space to pursue their interests.

Encouraging and celebrating each other's accomplishments and milestones

Encouraging and celebrating each other's accomplishments and milestones is important to a healthy and supportive relationship.

Here are some ways to encourage and celebrate your partner's accomplishments and milestones:

1. Show genuine interest: Be genuinely interested in your partner's accomplishments and milestones. Ask questions and actively listen to their stories and experiences.
2. Provide encouragement and support: Offer encouragement and support to your partner, especially when facing challenges or setbacks.
3. Celebrate the small wins: Celebrate even the smallest accomplishments and milestones, as they can be important stepping stones to larger goals.
4. Give thoughtful gifts: Surprise your partner with a thoughtful gift that reflects their accomplishment or milestone, such as a congratulatory card, a special dinner or outing, or a meaningful piece of jewelry.
5. Plan a special celebration: Plan a special celebration to mark a significant milestone, such as a graduation, a promotion, or a big achievement.
6. Express pride and admiration: Let your partner know how proud and admiring you are of their accomplishments and milestones. Expressing pride and admiration can be a powerful motivator for continued growth and achievement.

You can create a positive and supportive environment that fosters personal growth and relationship health by encouraging and celebrating each other's accomplishments and milestones. It can also help to deepen your bond and strengthen your connection as a couple.

USEFUL RESOURCES FOR SUPPORTING INDIVIDUAL GROWTH IN RELATIONSHIPS

A. BOOKS:

i. "The Dance of Anger: A Woman's Guide to Changing the Patterns of Intimate Relationships" by Harriet Lerner

"The Dance of Anger: A Woman's Guide to Changing the Patterns of Intimate Relationships" by Harriet Lerner is a self-help book for women who struggle with anger and relationships.

The book explores how women often suppress their anger in relationships and how this can lead to feelings of powerlessness and dissatisfaction. Lerner argues that anger is a natural and necessary emotion that can be used to create positive change in relationships.

The book is divided into three parts. Part One explores the nature of anger, why women often struggle with expressing anger, and the different ways that anger can be expressed in relationships. Part Two focuses on the specific patterns of behavior that can perpetuate conflicts, such as blaming, placating, and denying. Lerner provides practical advice and strategies for changing these patterns of behavior. Part Three explores how women can develop effective communication skills, set boundaries, and create healthier relationships.

ii. "Passionate Marriage: Keeping Love and Intimacy Alive in Committed Relationships" by David Schnarch

"Passionate Marriage: Keeping Love and Intimacy Alive in Committed Relationships" by David Schnarch is a book about how couples can maintain intimacy and passion in their long-term relationships.

The book is divided into three parts. Part One introduces the concept of differentiation, which Schnarch defines as maintaining one's individuality while staying emotionally connected to one's partner. Part Two explores how to deal with conflicts and balance individual needs with the relationship's needs. Schnarch provides practical advice and strategies for couples struggling with these issues.

Part Three focuses on sexuality and intimacy in long-term relationships. Schnarch argues that sexuality is a natural and important part of a healthy relationship and that maintaining intimacy and passion requires ongoing effort and attention.

The book emphasizes the importance of differentiation and encourages couples to take responsibility for their emotional well-being while staying emotionally connected to their partner.

iii. "The Power of Two: Secrets of a Strong and Loving Marriage" by Susan Heitler

"The Power of Two: Secrets of a Strong and Loving Marriage" by Susan Heitler is a book that focuses on the skills and tools that couples need to build and maintain a strong and loving relationship.

The book is divided into four parts. Part One discusses the importance of communication in a relationship and provides practical tips for improving communication skills. Part Two focuses on problem-solving and conflict resolution and provides strategies for resolving conflicts constructively and positively.

Part Three explores the issue of power dynamics in relationships and provides strategies for creating a balanced and equal partnership. Heitler argues that a healthy relationship requires a balance of power and that both partners need to feel valued and respected.

Part Four focuses on intimacy and sexuality in relationships and provides strategies for maintaining a healthy and satisfying sex life. Heitler emphasizes the importance of open communication and honesty in maintaining intimacy and provides practical tips for improving sexual communication and intimacy.

"The Power of Two" is a helpful resource for couples building and maintaining a strong and loving relationship. The book provides practical tools and strategies for improving communication, resolving conflicts, creating a balanced partnership, and maintaining intimacy and passion.

B. Podcasts:

i. "The One You Feed" by Eric Zimmer

"The One You Feed" is a podcast hosted by Eric Zimmer that explores the topics of personal growth, spirituality, and mental health. The podcast comes from a Native American parable about the battle between two wolves within us – one representing darkness, negativity, and despair, and the other representing light, positivity, and hope. The parable suggests that the wolf that wins is one we feed, and Zimmer uses this metaphor to explore how we can cultivate the habits, attitudes, and beliefs that lead to a more fulfilling and meaningful life.

Each episode of "The One You Feed" features an interview with a different expert or author on personal growth and mental health. Zimmer asks thoughtful and insightful questions that elicit practical advice and wisdom from his guests. The conversations cover many topics, including mindfulness, meditation, addiction, depression, anxiety, relationships, etc.

ii. "The Life Coach School Podcast" by Brooke Castillo

"The Life Coach School Podcast" is a popular self-help podcast by Brooke Castillo. The podcast focuses on personal development and provides practical strategies for overcoming common challenges in life, such as anxiety, procrastination, and self-doubt.

Each episode features a topic related to personal growth and well-being, and Castillo provides in-depth insights and actionable advice on overcoming specific issues. She also shares her personal experiences and stories, which adds a relatable and authentic tone to the podcast.

Some of the recurring themes on the podcast include self-awareness, emotional management, goal-setting, and mindset shifts. The podcast is geared towards individuals interested in personal development, whether they want to overcome specific challenges or improve their overall well-being.

C. Online courses and workshops:

i. The Optimal Living 101 Master Class by Brian Johnson

The Optimal Living 101 Master Class is an online course developed by Brian Johnson, a writer, philosopher, and entrepreneur. The course is designed to help participants optimize their lives by developing habits and practices that lead to greater happiness, success, and well-being.

The course is divided into 101 modules, each focusing on a specific topic related to personal growth and development. The modules cover many topics, including mindfulness, gratitude, goal-setting, and time management.

The course includes video lessons, audio lectures, and written materials that provide in-depth explanations of the concepts and practices covered in each module. In addition, the course includes worksheets, exercises, and challenges that allow participants to apply the concepts and practices to their own lives.

One of the unique features of the Optimal Living 101 Master Class is the emphasis on scientific research and evidence-based practices. Each module is grounded in research from fields such as positive psychology, neuroscience, and behavioral economics, providing participants with a solid foundation for understanding the concepts and practices.

The course also includes a community forum where participants can connect with each other, share their experiences, and receive support and encouragement. In addition, participants can schedule one-on-one coaching sessions with Brian Johnson, providing personalized guidance and support as they work through the course.

D. Apps:

i. Insight Timer

Insight Timer is a popular meditation app that offers various guided meditations, music tracks, and other resources to support meditation, mindfulness, and personal growth.

One of the key features of Insight Timer is the large library of guided meditations and talks from various teachers and experts in the field of meditation and mindfulness. Users can browse by topic, teacher, or duration, and meditations are available for beginners and more experienced practitioners. In addition, the app includes a timer feature that allows users to set their meditation session length and customize the sounds and background for their practice.

Insight Timer also includes other resources for personal growth and well-being, such as daily reminders, inspirational quotes, and articles on mindfulness and meditation. In addition, the app also offers courses on topics such as stress reduction, sleep improvement, and developing mindfulness practices in daily life.

The app also has a community aspect, with users able to connect with each other, share their experiences, and join groups and challenges focused on specific topics or practices. Users can also track their progress and see stats such as total meditation time and streaks.

ii. Goodreads

Goodreads is a social networking and book discovery platform that allows users to discover, rate, and review books and connect with other readers and authors. It is one of the largest online communities for book lovers, with over 90 million members and a vast database of books, reviews, and recommendations.

Goodreads users can create profiles, add friends, and join groups based on their reading preferences or interests. The platform also allows users to track the books they have read, want to read, or are currently reading and to rate and review books based on a five-star rating system. The platform also offers personalized recommendations based on the user's reading history and preferences.

One of the key features of Goodreads is its book recommendation system, which uses data such as the user's reading history, ratings, and reviews to suggest new books that they may enjoy. The platform also hosts author interviews, giveaways, and book clubs, allowing users to interact with their favorite authors and other readers.

Overall, Goodreads is a valuable resource for book lovers looking to discover new books, connect with other readers, and track their reading progress.

Supporting individual growth in a relationship is important because it allows each partner to develop a sense of identity and independence, leading to a healthier and more fulfilling relationship. In addition, when partners are encouraged to pursue their personal goals and interests, they are more likely to feel happy and fulfilled, strengthening their overall relationship.

Moreover, supporting individual growth can lead to greater emotional intimacy and deeper connections within the relationship. When partners can share their personal experiences and challenges with each other, they can create a more meaningful and authentic bond.

Ultimately, supporting individual growth in a relationship is about creating a space where both partners can thrive while maintaining a strong and healthy connection with each other. This can lead to a more fulfilling and satisfying relationship for both partners. Following the techniques and applying the activities can foster individual growth in your relationship and experience its various benefits.

WEEK 11: PLANNING FOR THE FUTURE

Planning for the future in a relationship means setting common goals, making joint decisions, and envisioning a shared future together. It involves discussing and planning important life milestones like marriage, children, career changes, and retirement.

By planning for the future together, couples can ensure they are on the same page regarding their shared goals and aspirations. This helps avoid misunderstandings or conflicts that may arise if partners have different expectations about what they want their future to look like.

Additionally, planning for the future of a relationship can build a sense of security and stability within the relationship. Partners can create a stronger sense of trust and mutual support by making joint decisions and commitments.

Some examples of planning for the future in a relationship include:

- Discussing long-term career goals and making education or training plans to help achieve those goals.
- Setting financial goals and creating a plan for saving money and managing debt.
- Discussing and planning for major life events, such as having children or buying a home.
- Making decisions about where to live and how to divide household responsibilities.
- Planning for retirement and discussing goals for travel, hobbies, and other activities.

Revisiting Shared Goals and Values

Over time, people's priorities and interests can change, and it's important for couples to periodically check in with each other to make sure they're still aligned and working towards common goals.

Identifying shared goals and values is one of the first steps in revisiting them. Next, couples can discuss and write down their shared goals and values and their individual ones to see where there might be overlaps or differences.

Couples need to discuss how they can work towards those shared goals and values together. This might involve setting specific action steps or milestones or brainstorming ways to support each other in achieving those goals.

It's also important to recognize that priorities and values may change over time, and that's okay. However, if there are differences, it's important to have open and honest communication about those differences and find ways to compromise or find common ground.

Revisiting shared goals and values can strengthen a relationship by creating a sense of shared purpose and direction. It also helps build trust and understanding between partners as they work towards common goals and support each other in achieving them.

Reflecting on the Progress Made During the 8-Week Program

Reflecting on the progress made during an 8-week program can be a helpful way to assess how much you have grown and changed during that time. Here are some steps you can take to reflect on your progress:

1. Review your initial goals: At the beginning of the program, you likely set some goals for yourself. Look back at those goals and evaluate how much progress you have made towards achieving them.
2. Identify your strengths: Take some time to think about what you have learned about yourself and what strengths you have developed during the program.
3. Acknowledge challenges: Consider the challenges you faced during the program and how you overcame them.
4. Evaluate your mindset: Consider how your mindset may have shifted during the program. For example, have you developed a more positive outlook or become more open to new experiences?
5. Evaluate your relationships: Reflect on how your relationships may have changed during the program. For example, have you developed stronger connections with others or improved communication with your loved ones?
6. Consider future goals: Finally, consider what you want to achieve. How can you build on your progress during the program and continue to grow and improve?

Another approach to assessing your progress is through questions. In this segment, find time to be with your partner and discuss some of these questions:

1. What important things have we learned about each other, like pet peeves, likes, dislikes, and triggers?
2. What improvements have we observed in our relationship so far?
3. What growth have we experienced as individuals and as a couple?

4. How have our communication and conflict-resolution skills improved?
5. What specific exercises or strategies have been most helpful to us?
6. What challenges have we encountered during therapy, and how have we overcome them?
7. How can we better support each other's goals and dreams?
8. What are some things we can do to strengthen our emotional connection?
9. How can we improve our communication with each other?
10. What are some things we do that create conflict, and how can we address them?
11. What shared interests or activities can we pursue together?
12. How can we show appreciation and gratitude for each other?
13. What are some ways we can prioritize quality time together?
14. How can we ensure we meet each other's needs in the relationship?
15. How can we better manage stress and conflict in our relationship?
16. Finally, how can we keep romance and passion alive in our relationship?

Reflecting on your progress can help you appreciate how far you have come and feel more confident in your ability to continue progressing. It can also help you identify areas where you may want to focus more on to continue growing and developing.

Reassessing and adjusting goals and values as needed

As individuals and couples evolve, their goals and values may also change. It's important to regularly reflect on these changes and make any necessary adjustments to ensure that both partners feel fulfilled and supported in the relationship.

When reassessing goals and values, it can be helpful to ask questions such as:

- Are our current goals and values aligned with our individual and collective growth?
- Are we still working towards the same goals, or have our priorities shifted?
- Are there any values that we need to re-evaluate or clarify?
- Are there any new goals or values that we want to add to our list?

Once these questions have been answered, it's important to communicate openly and honestly with your partner about any changes or adjustments that need to be made.

It's also important to remember that goals and values can be fluid and change over time. As such, it's important to regularly revisit and reassess them to ensure both partners are growing and evolving.

CREATING A RELATIONSHIP VISION AND MISSION STATEMENT

Creating a vision for a relationship can help clarify and communicate the goals and values of the partnership. Here are some steps to create a relationship vision:

1. Begin by having an open and honest discussion with your partner about what you want your relationship to be like. Talk about your shared values, goals, and dreams for the future.
2. Write down the values that are most important to both of you. These can include honesty, respect, communication, trust, and commitment.
3. Your vision should define what you want to achieve as a couple. For example, it might include goals such as building a strong foundation of trust, deepening your emotional connection, and supporting each other's personal growth.
4. Your vision statement should paint a picture of the relationship you want to create. For example, it might include a shared vision of your future together, such as building a happy home and family.
5. Once you have identified your shared values, defined your mission, and crafted your vision statement, write it down in a clear and concise way.
6. Your vision statement should be a living document that evolves. Make sure to review it regularly with your partner and revise it as needed to reflect changes in your goals, values, and relationship dynamics.

DEFINING THE IDEAL RELATIONSHIP AND WHAT IT MEANS TO BOTH PARTNERS

Defining the ideal relationship is a highly personal and individual process that varies from couple to couple. However, some common themes can help guide the process of defining an ideal relationship. Here are some steps to defining the ideal relationship and what it means to both partners:

1. Identify your values: Values are the principles that guide our lives and play a critical role in defining the ideal relationship. Both partners should identify their values and then discuss which values they share and which are most important to them as a couple.

2. Discuss your needs: Needs are the things that we require to feel fulfilled and satisfied in a relationship. Both partners should identify their needs and then discuss which ones they share. Common needs in a healthy relationship include emotional support, physical affection, intellectual stimulation, and shared interests.
3. Define your boundaries: Boundaries are the limits we set to protect ourselves and our relationships. Common boundaries in a healthy relationship include respecting each other's privacy, maintaining individual identities, and not engaging in harmful behaviors.
4. Discuss your goals: Goals are what we want to achieve in a relationship, both individually and as a couple. Common goals in a healthy relationship include building a strong foundation of trust, deepening emotional intimacy, and supporting each other's personal growth.
5. Create a shared vision: Using the information gathered from the previous steps, both partners can create a shared vision of the ideal relationship. This vision should reflect the values, needs, boundaries, and goals most important to both partners. It should be a positive, inspiring, and realistic picture of what the couple wants to achieve together.
6. Continuously communicate and adapt: Both partners should regularly discuss their progress toward their shared vision, as well as any changes in their values, needs, boundaries, or goals. This will help ensure the relationship remains healthy, fulfilling, and aligned with both partners' needs and aspirations.

In summary, defining the ideal relationship requires identifying individual values, needs, boundaries, and goals and creating a shared vision reflecting both partners' aspirations. Regular communication and adaptation are key to ensuring that the relationship remains healthy and fulfilling for both partners.

Establishing a Vision Board or Visual Representation of Your Relationship Goals

Establishing a vision board or visual representation of your relationship goals can be a fun and effective way to bring your shared values and objectives to life. Here are some steps to creating a vision board or visual representation of your relationship goals:

1. Reflect on your shared goals: Review your joint mission statement and discuss the specific goals and objectives you have set for your relationship.
2. Gather inspiration: Look for images, words, and symbols representing your shared goals and objectives.

3. Select your medium: Decide whether you want to create a physical vision board using a poster board, cork board, collage, or a digital one using online tools like Pinterest or Canva.
4. Create your vision board: Using your chosen medium, start selecting and arranging the images, words, and symbols that represent your shared goals and objectives. Make sure to include both short-term and long-term goals and arrange them in a way that feels meaningful and inspiring to both partners.
5. Display your vision board: Once you have created it, display it in your bedroom, living room, or home office. The visual representation of your relationship goals will serve as a reminder of your shared values and objectives. In addition, it can keep you motivated and focused on your relationship journey.
6. Regularly review and update your vision board: Make sure to regularly review and update your vision board to reflect changes in your goals, values, and relationship dynamics.

Remember that creating a vision board or visual representation of your relationship goals is a creative and personal process and should be tailored to your unique values and objectives as a couple. Have fun with it, and use it as a tool to inspire and motivate both partners toward a happy and fulfilling relationship.

Preparing for Potential Challenges and Setbacks

Discussing Possible Future Stressors and Obstacles

Discussing possible future stressors and obstacles is important in any relationship because it allows couples to anticipate and prepare for possible challenges. By having open and honest conversations about potential stressors and obstacles, couples can develop strategies to address them and minimize their impact on the relationship.

Here are some benefits of discussing possible future stressors and obstacles:

1. Encourages teamwork: Discussing potential stressors and obstacles can encourage couples to work together as a team to address challenges. This can help build a stronger partnership and foster a sense of mutual support.
2. Reduces conflict: Couples can identify potential areas of conflict and work proactively to address them. This can help reduce conflict and tension in the relationship.
3. Increases trust: Discussing potential stressors and obstacles can increase trust between partners by demonstrating a willingness to be open and honest about potential challenges.

4. Promotes problem-solving skills: Couples can develop problem-solving skills that can help them address challenges in the future.

Determining possible stressors and obstacles in a relationship involves identifying areas of potential conflict or challenges that may arise. Here are some steps couples can take to identify possible stressors and obstacles in their relationship:

1. Reflect on past challenges: Consider any past challenges or conflicts that have arisen in the relationship. These provide insight into areas that could be potential stressors in the future.
2. Discuss individual stressors: Each partner should discuss any personal or professional stressors or challenges they may face that could impact the relationship.
3. Consider life changes: Changes in life circumstances, for example, moving, starting a new job, or having a child, can be potential stressors for the relationship. Discuss any upcoming life changes and how they may impact the relationship.
4. Identify communication challenges: Communication challenges, like, disagreements about how to communicate or difficulty expressing emotions, can be potential stressors for the relationship. Identify any communication challenges and work together to address them.
5. Discuss expectations: Different expectations around areas such as finances, household chores, and social activities can be potential stressors for the relationship. Discuss any expectations and work together to find common ground.
6. Explore differences in values and beliefs: Differences in values and beliefs can lead to conflict and stress in a relationship. Identify any differences and work together to find ways to respect and navigate them.

By taking these steps to identify potential stressors and obstacles in the relationship, couples can develop strategies to address them and minimize their impact on the relationship.

Creating a plan for handling difficult situations together

Creating a plan for handling difficult situations together can help couples navigate challenging times and strengthen their relationship. Here are some steps to create a plan for handling difficult situations together:

1. Discuss individual strengths and weaknesses: Each partner should discuss their individual strengths and weaknesses and how they can best contribute to handling difficult situations. This can help create a sense of teamwork and mutual support.

2. Define roles and responsibilities: Depending on the nature of the challenge, it may be helpful to define specific roles and responsibilities for each partner. For example, one partner may be responsible for handling finances, while the other may be responsible for managing household tasks.
3. Develop a communication plan: Clear communication is essential when handling difficult situations. Therefore, couples should develop a communication plan that outlines how they will keep each other informed and make decisions together.
4. Identify external resources: Depending on the nature of the challenge, it may be helpful to identify external resources that can provide support, such as a therapist or financial advisor.
5. Review and update the plan regularly: As circumstances change, it's important to review and update the plan regularly to ensure it remains relevant and effective.

Creating a plan for handling difficult situations together can help couples feel more prepared and confident in their ability to navigate challenges. It can also foster a sense of mutual support and teamwork, which can strengthen the relationship overall.

Identifying and Committing to Resources That Can Provide Ongoing Support

Identifying and committing to resources that can provide ongoing support is important in maintaining a healthy and strong relationship. Here are some types of resources that couples can consider:

1. Couples therapy can provide a safe and supportive space for couples to work through challenges and improve their communication and problem-solving skills.
2. Joining a support group can allow couples to connect with others going through similar experiences and gain support and perspective.
3. Many books, online courses, and other educational resources can provide valuable insights and strategies for maintaining a healthy relationship.
4. Identifying couples who have strong and healthy relationships and seeking their guidance and advice can be a valuable resource.
5. Individual therapy can provide a supportive space for each partner to work through personal challenges that may be impacting the relationship.

6. For spiritual or religious couples, seeking support from their community or leaders can provide valuable guidance and perspective.

It's important for couples to identify the resources that best meet their needs and commit to utilizing them as needed. Ongoing support and guidance can help couples navigate challenges and maintain a strong and healthy relationship over time.

Ongoing Maintenance and Growth

Establishing Regular Relationship Check-ins or "State of the Union" Meetings

Regular relationship check-ins are a proactive way for couples to prevent problems from escalating and address any concerns or issues before they become major problems. Here are some tips for establishing regular relationship check-ins:

1. Set a regular time and place: Schedule a regular time and place for your check-ins, such as a weekly or monthly meeting, in a quiet and private space where you can focus on your conversation.
2. Use a structured approach: Use a structured approach to guide your conversation and ensure that you cover all the important topics. This could include discussing what's been going well, areas for improvement, and any concerns or challenges.
3. Practice active listening: Practice active listening during your check-ins, which means fully focusing on your partner's words without interrupting or being defensive.
4. Stay positive: Keep your check-ins positive and solution-focused. Focus on working together to overcome challenges and celebrate your successes.
5. Follow through on action items: Identify them during your check-ins and make sure you follow through on them. This will help build trust and show your commitment to the relationship.

Regular relationship check-ins can help prevent small problems from turning into bigger ones and can help strengthen the overall relationship. By setting aside time to communicate regularly and address concerns, couples can build a stronger foundation for their relationship and increase their overall satisfaction and happiness together.

Setting aside time for regular date nights and bonding activities

Setting aside time for regular date nights and bonding activities is an important way to strengthen the connection and intimacy in a relationship. Here are some tips for establishing regular date nights and bonding activities:

1. Schedule it in advance: Set aside a specific time in your calendar each week or month for your date night or bonding activity. This will help ensure that you both prioritize this time together.
2. Mix it up: Try a variety of activities to keep things interesting and avoid falling into a routine. This could include trying new restaurants, taking a dance class, going on a hike, or attending a concert or movie.
3. Unplug and disconnect: Avoid distractions like phones or computers during your date night or bonding activity. This will allow you to focus on each other and strengthen your connection.
4. Communicate openly: Use this time to communicate openly and honestly with each other. Share your thoughts, feelings, and experiences to deepen your understanding of each other.
5. Have fun: Make sure to have fun and enjoy each other's company. Laughter and playfulness can help build a positive and enjoyable experience.

Regular date nights and bonding activities can help couples maintain a strong connection and keep the spark alive in their relationship. In addition, couples can deepen their bond and enjoy a fulfilling and happy relationship by making time for each other, trying new things, and communicating openly.

Continuing to invest in personal growth and self-care

Continuing to invest in personal growth and self-care is important for individuals in a relationship as it allows them to maintain their individual identities and avoid becoming too dependent on their partner. Here are some tips for investing in personal growth and self-care:

1. Pursue hobbies and interests: Take time to pursue hobbies and interests that bring you joy and fulfillment. This will help you maintain a sense of self outside of your relationship.
2. Set personal goals: Set personal goals for yourself and work towards achieving them. This will help you continue to grow and develop as an individual.
3. Practice self-care: Prioritize self-care activities such as exercise, meditation, and relaxation techniques. This will help you manage stress and maintain your physical and emotional well-being.

4. Seek support: Seek support from friends, family, or a therapist if needed. This will help you work through any personal challenges and maintain a healthy perspective on your relationship.
5. Communicate with your partner: Communicate openly with your partner about your personal growth and self-care journey. Share your goals and progress, and encourage your partner to do the same.

Investing in personal growth and self-care can help individuals maintain a healthy sense of self and avoid becoming too dependent on their partner for happiness and fulfillment. By prioritizing personal growth and self-care, individuals can bring their best selves to the relationship and contribute to its overall health and success.

USEFUL RESOURCES FOR MAINTAINING AND GROWING YOUR RELATIONSHIP

A. BOOKS:

i. "Eight Dates: Essential Conversations for a Lifetime of Love" by John Gottman and Julie Schwartz Gottman

"Eight Dates: Essential Conversations for a Lifetime of Love" is a book by John Gottman and Julie Schwartz Gottman. It offers a practical guide for couples who want to strengthen their relationship. The book is based on research conducted by the Gottmans and is designed to help couples have meaningful conversations about important topics that are often overlooked or avoided.

The book is divided into eight chapters, each focusing on a specific important topic for building a strong relationship. The topics covered include trust and commitment, conflict resolution, sex and intimacy, work and money, family, fun and adventure, growth and spirituality, and dreams.

Each chapter provides exercises and conversation starters for couples to engage in meaningful discussions. The exercises help couples better understand each other, communicate more effectively, and build a deeper connection.

One of the unique aspects of "Eight Dates" is that it encourages couples to set aside time for intentional conversations about their relationship. The book suggests that couples go on eight dates, each focused on one of the topics covered in the book. The authors believe these intentional conversations can help couples build a strong foundation for a lifetime of love.

ii. "The Relationship Cure: A 5-Step Guide to Strengthening Your Marriage, Family, and Friendships" by John Gottman

"The Relationship Cure: A 5-Step Guide to Strengthening Your Marriage, Family, and Friendships" is a book by John Gottman that focuses on improving communication and building stronger relationships. Gottman is a renowned psychologist and researcher who has spent decades studying relationships and identifying the factors contributing to their success or failure.

In "The Relationship Cure," Gottman presents a five-step approach to building stronger relationships. The steps are:

1. Recognizing when a relationship is in trouble: The first step is to recognize when a relationship is in trouble and identify the negative patterns of interaction causing problems.
2. Learning to calm down: The second step is to learn how to calm down when emotions are running high. Gottman provides techniques for managing stress and reducing conflict.
3. Practicing emotional attunement: The third step is to practice emotional attunement, which involves paying attention to your partner's emotions and responding in a supportive way.
4. Building positive interactions: The fourth step is to build positive interactions by focusing on shared interests, creating rituals of connection, and showing appreciation for your partner.
5. Finding shared meaning: The final step is to find shared meaning in your relationship by identifying shared values and goals.

Gottman provides practical exercises, and techniques couples can use to strengthen their relationships throughout the book. He also shares stories and examples from his clinical practice to illustrate the principles he presents.

B. Podcasts:

i. "Where Should We Begin?" by Esther Perel

"Where Should We Begin?" is a podcast by Esther Perel, a world-renowned therapist, speaker, and author specializing in couples therapy and relationship dynamics. The podcast offers listeners an intimate and unfiltered look into real-life couples therapy sessions.

In each episode, Perel shares a recorded therapy session with a couple struggling with a particular issue in their relationship. The sessions are raw and emotional, with the couple sharing their deepest fears and desires with Perel as she guides them through understanding and communicating with each other.

The topics covered in "Where Should We Begin?" are wide-ranging, including infidelity, communication breakdowns, sexual desire, and cultural differences. Perel's unique approach to therapy emphasizes empathy, understanding, and communication, and she often challenges traditional notions of monogamy and romantic love.

One of the most compelling aspects of the podcast is how Perel uses her experiences and insights to guide the couples she works with. She draws on her extensive knowledge of psychology, sociology, and anthropology to help couples understand the complex dynamics at play in their relationship.

C. Online courses and workshops:

i. The Art and Science of Love by The Gottman Institute (advanced workshops)

"The Art and Science of Love" is a series of advanced workshops offered by The Gottman Institute, a research-based organization dedicated to improving relationships through education and therapy. The workshops are designed to help couples deepen their understanding of each other and learn practical skills for building a strong and lasting relationship.

The workshops are based on the research of Drs. John and Julie Gottman, who are world-renowned experts in the field of couples therapy and relationship research. The workshops are designed to provide couples with an immersive experience beyond traditional couples therapy.

The workshop covers topics such as emotional intelligence, conflict resolution, and communication skills. Participants are given practical tools and techniques for improving their relationship and an opportunity to practice these skills with their partner in a supportive and constructive environment.

In addition to the core workshop, advanced workshops focus on specific topics such as intimacy, parenting, and trust. These workshops provide couples with more in-depth knowledge and tools for addressing specific challenges in their relationship.

Overall, "The Art and Science of Love" workshops are highly regarded in couples therapy and have helped thousands of couples worldwide build stronger and more fulfilling relationships. The workshops are led by experienced therapists trained in the Gottman Method, based on decades of research into what makes relationships successful.

ii. Hold Me Tight Online by Dr. Sue Johnson (advanced modules)

"Hold Me Tight Online" is a series of advanced modules offered by Dr. Sue Johnson, the creator of Emotionally Focused Therapy (EFT). EFT is a type of couples therapy that focuses on helping couples create a stronger emotional bond by improving their ability to communicate and understand each other's needs.

The "Hold Me Tight Online" modules are designed to build on the principles of EFT and help couples deepen their understanding of each other. The modules cover topics such as attachment styles, emotional regulation, and communication skills. The modules are delivered through an online platform and include instructional videos, exercises, and discussions with other couples.

The advanced modules are designed for couples who have already completed the basic Hold Me Tight program or have experience with EFT therapy. The advanced modules cover more complex topics such as trauma, infidelity, and chronic relationship issues. These modules aim to help couples identify and address the deeper emotional issues that may be impacting their relationship.

Dr. Sue Johnson is a well-respected expert in couples therapy and has written several books on the subject, including "Hold Me Tight" and "Love Sense." The "Hold Me Tight Online" program is based on her extensive research and clinical experience. It has helped thousands of couples strengthen their emotional connection and build more fulfilling relationships worldwide.

In the end, remember every relationship is unique, and finding the strategies and activities that work best for you and your partner is important. Don't be afraid to try new things, and be open to feedback and suggestions from each other. Committing to working on your relationship can create a healthier and more fulfilling partnership.

Made in the USA
Las Vegas, NV
10 September 2023

77397952R00105